QUESTION YOUR THINKING,

CHANGE THE WORLD

ALSO BY BYRON KATIE

A Thousand Names for Joy (with Stephen Mitchell)

I Need Your Love—Is That True?
(with Michael Katz)

Loving What Is (with Stephen Mitchell)

All of the above are available at your local
bookstore, or may be ordered by visiting:

Hay House USA: **www.hayhouse.com**®
Hay House Australia: **www.hayhouse.com.au**
Hay House UK: **www.hayhouse.co.uk**
Hay House South Africa: **www.hayhouse.co.za**
Hay House India: **www.hayhouse.co.in**

PRAISE FOR BYRON KATIE AND THE WORK

"A spiritual innovator for the new millennium. The charismatic Katie acts as a combination mystical guide, wise-cracking therapist and knowing parent."

— *Time* magazine

"Katie's laser-like tough love burns away all illusions."

— *The Times* (London)

"Byron Katie's Work is a great blessing for our planet. It acts like a razor-sharp sword that cuts through illusions and enables you to know for yourself the timeless essence of your being."

— **Eckhart Tolle**, author of *The Power of Now*

"Suppose you could find a simple way to embrace your life with joy, and achieve serenity in the midst of chaos? That is what Katie offers. It is no less than a revolutionary way to live your life. The question is: are we brave enough to accept it?"

— **Erica Jong**, author of *Fear of Flying*

"Katie's Work is a wonderful, transformative practice for anyone interested in spiritual growth."

— **Lama Surya Das**, author of *Awakening the Buddha Within*

QUESTION
YOUR THINKING,

CHANGE
THE WORLD

Quotations from
BYRON KATIE

EDITED BY STEPHEN MITCHELL

HAY HOUSE, INC.
Carlsbad, California • New York City
London • Sydney • Johannesburg
Vancouver • Hong Kong • New Delhi

Published and distributed in the United States by: Hay House, Inc.: www.hayhouse.com • **Published and distributed in Australia by:** Hay House Australia Pty. Ltd.: www.hayhouse.com.au • **Published and distributed in the United Kingdom by:** Hay House UK, Ltd.: www.hayhouse.co.uk • **Published and distributed in the Republic of South Africa by:** Hay House SA (Pty), Ltd. • www.hayhouse.co.za • **Distributed in Canada by:** Raincoast: www.raincoast.com • **Published in India by:** Hay House Publishers India: www.hayhouse.co.in

Design: Tricia Breidenthal

Some of the passages in this book first appeared in Byron Katie's *Loving What Is* and *A Thousand Names for Joy,* and are reprinted by permission of Harmony Books.

Library of Congress Cataloging-in-Publication Data

Katie, Byron.
  Question your thinking, change the world : quotations from Byron Katie
/ edited by Stephen Mitchell. -- 1st ed.
      p. cm.
  ISBN-13: 978-1-4019-1730-2 (tradepaper) 1. Conduct of life--
Quotations, maxims, etc. 2. Self-acceptance. 3. Reality. I. Mitchell,
Stephen, 1943- II. Title.
  BJ1581.2.K34 2007
  158--dc22

                                    2006029473

ISBN: 978-1-4019-1730-2

10 09 08 07   5 4 3 2
1st edition, October 2007
2nd edition, October 2007

Printed in the United States of America

To Bob, Dana,
Ross, Roxann, and Scott

CONTENTS

INTRODUCTION

The quotations in this book are just reminders. The fact is that you are the wisdom you've been seeking. My experience is that we all have equal wisdom, and there is no one with more wisdom than you.

You can find that wisdom by doing The Work (which I describe below). It's a way to go inside and tap into your wisdom whenever you want. If you think that you have a problem, you're confused. Go inside and know what's true for you: that is the medicine, that is the freedom. It's the freedom I enjoy.

What I love about The Work is that it allows you to go inside and experience your own freedom for yourself, to experience what already exists within you: the wisdom that is unchanging, immovable, ever waiting, ever present. The Work allows you to go there. It's like going home. You don't need a teacher.

To ask is to receive, and now you know what to ask. Don't wait for the answer of anyone else, and don't believe a word I say. Give yourself your own wisdom. You create your own suffering, and you can end it. It's as simple as that.

ABOUT THE WORK

The Work is a simple yet powerful process of inquiry that teaches you to identify and question the stressful thoughts that cause all the suffering in the world. It consists of four questions that you apply to a stressful thought. It's a way to understand what's hurting you, a way to end all your stress and suffering. It works for everyone who is open to it, and it has a profound effect on your whole life. It will affect not only your own life, but your partner's life and the lives of your children and your children's children.

A thought is harmless unless we believe it. It's not our thoughts, but the *attachment* to our thoughts, that causes suffering. Attaching to a thought means believing that it's true, without inquiring. A belief is a thought that we've been attaching to, often for years.

Most people think that they are what their thoughts tell them they are. One day I noticed that I wasn't breathing—I was being breathed. Then I also noticed, to my amazement, that I wasn't thinking—that I was actually being thought and that thinking isn't personal. Do you wake up in the morning and say to yourself, "I think I won't think today"? It's too late: you're already thinking! Thoughts just appear. They come out of nothing and go back to nothing, like clouds moving across the empty sky. They come to pass, not to stay. There is no harm in them until we attach to them as if they were true.

No one has ever been able to control their thinking, although people may tell the story of how they have. I don't let go of my thoughts—I meet them with understanding, then *they* let go of *me*.

PUTTING THE MIND ON PAPER

The first step in The Work is to write down your stressful thoughts about any situation in your life, past, present, or future—about a person you dislike or a situation with someone who angers or frightens or saddens you. (There's a sample Judge-Your-Neighbor Worksheet in *Loving What Is*, or you can go to **www.TheWork.com** and download and print one.)

For thousands of years, we have been taught not to judge—but let's face it, we still do it all the time. The truth is that we all have judgments running in our heads. Through The Work, we finally have permission to let those judgments speak out, or even scream out, on paper. We may find that even the most unpleasant thoughts can be met with unconditional love.

I encourage you to write about someone whom you haven't yet totally forgiven. This is the most powerful place to begin. Even if you've forgiven that person 99 percent, you aren't free until your forgiveness is complete. That one percent you haven't forgiven is the very place where you're stuck in all your other relationships (including your relationship with yourself).

If you're new to The Work, I strongly suggest that you not write about yourself at first. If you start by judging yourself, your answers often come with old motives and with answers that don't work. Judging someone else, then inquiring and turning it around, is the direct path to freedom. You can judge yourself later, when you've been doing inquiry long enough to trust the power of your own truths.

If you begin by pointing the finger of blame outward, then the focus isn't on you. You can just let loose and be uncensored. We're often quite sure about what other people need to do, how they should live, and whom they should be with. We have 20/20 vision about others, but not about ourselves.

When you do The Work, you see who you are by seeing who you think other people are. Eventually you come to see that everything outside you is a reflection of your own thinking. You are the storyteller, the projector of all stories, and the world is the projected image of your thoughts.

Since the beginning of time, people have been trying to change the world so that they can be happy. This hasn't ever worked, because it approaches the problem backward. What The Work gives us is a way to change the projector—mind—rather than the projected. It's like when there's a piece of lint on a projector's lens. We think there's a flaw on the screen and we try to change this person and that person, whomever the flaw appears to be on next. But it's futile to try to change the projected images. Once we realize where the lint is, we can clear the lens itself. This is the end of suffering, and the beginning of a little joy in paradise.

FOUR QUESTIONS AND A TURNAROUND

The Work can be applied to any thought that causes you anger, fear, sadness, or frustration—any thought that keeps you from living in peace.

Thoughts such as "My mother doesn't love me," "My boss doesn't appreciate me," "I'm too fat," "I need to be healthier," "My children should obey me," or "My brother should stop drinking" pass through our minds many times a day. When you believe these thoughts, you suffer; but when you question them, you can discover what is really hurting you. Once you realize the difference between what is real and what is not, you naturally begin to act with clarity and efficiency and to live the life you always wanted to live.

After you've filled in the blanks on the Judge-Your-Neighbor Worksheet, you question each of your statements using the four questions of The Work, and then you turn the statement around. (The turnaround is a way of experiencing the opposite of what you believe.)

Stressful thought: "My husband doesn't listen to me."

The four questions:

1. Is it true?

2. Can you absolutely know that it's true?

3. How do you react when you believe that thought?

4. Who would you be without the thought?

Apply each of these four questions in turn to the stressful thought. Ask yourself the question, sit still, wait, and allow your answer to surface from deep within.

Once you've walked yourself through the four questions, turn the thought around by finding opposites to the statement you wrote. For example, "My husband doesn't listen to me." One turnaround is "My husband does listen to me." Find three genuine examples of how that statement is true in your life. There are other possible turnarounds, such as "I don't listen to me" and "I don't listen to my husband." Find three examples for each turnaround.

When you question your stressful thoughts, you come to see that everything that has been troubling you is just a misunderstanding. You realize that what you believe isn't necessarily so. This is the beginning of freedom. The Work always leaves you a kinder, clearer, happier human being.

ON LOVE, SEX, AND RELATIONSHIPS

Nothing outside you can ever give you what you're looking for.

Once we begin to question our thoughts, our partners—alive, dead, or divorced—are always our greatest teachers. There's no mistake about the person you're with; he or she is the perfect teacher for you, whether or not the relationship works out, and once you enter inquiry, you come to see that clearly.

There's never a mistake in the universe. So if your partner is angry, good. If there are things about him that you consider flaws, good, because these flaws are your own, you're projecting them, and you can write them down, inquire, and set yourself free. People go to India to find a guru, but you don't have to: you're living with one. Your partner will give you everything you need for your own freedom.

When you don't love the other person, it hurts, because love is your very self. And you can't *make* yourself do it! You can't make yourself love someone. But when you come to love yourself, you automatically love the other person. You can't not. Just as you can't make yourself love us, you can't make yourself not love us. It's all your projection.

Personalities don't love; they want something. Love doesn't seek anything. It's already complete. It doesn't want, doesn't need, has no *should*s (not even for the person's own good). So when I hear people say that they love someone and want to be loved in return, I know they're not talking about love. They're talking about something else.

2

I can't feel angry at my partner without suffering. This doesn't feel natural to me. It doesn't feel resonant. If I meet my partner with understanding, it feels more like me. So when a thought appears, can I meet that thought with understanding? When I've learned to meet my thoughts with understanding, I meet you with understanding.

What could you say about me that I haven't already thought? There *are* no new thoughts—they're all recycled. We're not meeting anything but thoughts. The external is the internal projected. Whether it's your thinking or my thinking, it's the same. Let's meet it with understanding. Only love heals.

It has been a life's work to make our partner wrong. Then when we enter inquiry, we lose. It's a tremendous shock. And it turns out to be grace. Winning is losing. Losing is winning. It all turns around.

When you own your share in something that your partner did to you, it's the sweetest thing in the world. You just feel humility, without the slightest urge to defend yourself. It leaves you completely vulnerable.

This is the kind of vulnerability you want to lick off the pavement, it's so delicious.

My love is *my* business; it has nothing to do with you. You love me, and that isn't personal. You tell the story that I am this, or I am that, and you fall in love with your story. What do I have to do with it? I am here for your perception, as if I had a choice. I am your story, no more and no less. You have never met me. No one has ever met anyone.

It's not your job to love me—it's mine.

When you believe the thought "My husband should understand me," and the reality is that he doesn't, it's a recipe for unhappiness. You can do everything in the world to make him understand you, and he'll end by understanding what he understands. And if he understands you, what do you have? Just validation that your story is true. What he says he understands isn't even you, because as you manipulate his understanding, he can only understand the story you're telling. So even at its best, you're not being understood. We don't hear what you tell us; we hear what we think you're telling us. We impose our story on what you say, and that's what we understand. Are your thoughts what you punish him for?

I love telling a story that happened around 1997, when I was traveling every day, sharing The Work with people all over the world, day after day, constantly on planes, trains, and in cars. One night I got on a plane and I was really exhausted. It was a red-eye; that's what I could afford. I sat down next to a man, picked up his hand, put it in my lap, and fell asleep. I had no qualms about it, because I knew what he really was, and I knew that he loved me, although we'd never met. He was still holding my hand when I woke up hours later. He was so sweet about it. He never asked my name.

But he wasn't any sweeter than the suitcase that fell from the overhead bin onto my head on another flight. It felt like a kiss as I collapsed. How do I know that I needed a hit on the head? Because that's what happened! No mistake. When you know that whatever you need is what you get, life becomes paradise. It's the perfect setup. Everything you need, and even more than you need, is always supplied, in abundance.

When I walk into a room, I know that everyone in it loves me. I just don't expect them to realize it yet.

The only possibility of being understood by someone else is to understand yourself. It's a full-time job. So if you inquire and come to see that what is is what you want, it's the end of any decisions about him. At that point you don't have to make any decision. There's no decision to torture him into understanding you. He continues to show you that his understanding is not your business.

What is an example that will prove that you aren't lovable? Rejection? If someone rejects you—and he could only do that because you don't match his beliefs about how he wants the world to be—it has nothing to do with you. Only an inflated ego could

6

say that it had anything to do with you. Suppose your hand just moved for no reason, and he turns himself off with what he believes that means—do you have the audacity to think that you had something to do with it? You don't have that power, ever. If he yells at you and you perceive that that isn't love, *you* have hurt yourself; he hasn't. And if you're yelling within you that he shouldn't yell at you, that is where the pain begins, not with his yelling at you. You're arguing with reality, and you lose.

When you say or do anything to please, get, keep, influence, or control anyone or anything, fear is the cause and pain is the result. Manipulation is separation, and separation is painful. Another person can love you totally in that moment and you'd have no way of realizing it. If you act from fear, there's no way you can receive love, because you're trapped in a thought about what you have to *do* for love. Every stressful thought separates you from people.

A dishonest yes is a no to yourself.

When a thought hurts, that's the signal that it isn't true.

Look at what you imagine is a flaw in your partner, and notice the ways that it gives you an opportunity to appreciate her. If you can't find these ways, you'll eventually have to strike out in anger—or you may just become frustrated by your lack of progress and attack yourself and her mentally. These attacks that you experience along the way are simply areas that need to be questioned, that's all. If the ways become obvious, you'll grow and grow into love without limit. And your partner will follow, and so will the rest of the world.

Reality unfolds perfectly. Whatever happens is good. I see people and things, and when it comes to me to move toward them or away from them, I move without argument, because I have no believable story about why I shouldn't; it's always perfect. A decision would give me less, always less. So "it" makes its own decision, and I follow. And what I love is that it's always kind. If I had to name the experience in a word, I would call it "gratitude." Living, breathing gratitude. I am a receiver, and there's nothing I can do to stop grace from coming in.

Seeking love is how you lose the awareness of love. But you can only lose the awareness of it, not the state. That is not an option, because love is what we all are. That's immovable. When you investigate your stressful thinking and your mind becomes clear, love pours into your life, and there's nothing you can do about it.

A friend sat in my room one morning—she's so courageous—with tears pouring down her face, saying, "I love you, Katie, I love you." The woman had no dignity. I saw her love for herself reflected through me. She saw that, too. And I said to her, "Isn't it fine to love at such a level and know you're not ever going to be disappointed in it?"

Sometimes you may appear to trade that love for the story appearing in the moment. It's like a little side-trip out into illusion. And when you investigate your story, you come back to where you always are.

When I don't look for approval outside me, I remain as approval. If I seek your approval, it's not comfortable inside me. And through inquiry, I've come to see that I want you to approve of what you approve of, because I love you. What you approve of is what I want. That's love—it wouldn't change anything. It already has everything it wants. It already *is* everything it wants, just the way it wants it.

All the advice you ever gave your partner is for you to hear.

Your partner is your mirror. Except for the way you perceive him, he doesn't even exist for you. He is who you see he is, and ultimately it's just you again, thinking. It's just you, over and over and over and over, and in this way you remain blind to yourself and feel justified and lost. To think that your partner is anything but a mirror of you is painful. You don't see your partner; you just see what you believe about him. So when you see him as flawed in any way, you can be sure that that's where your own flaw is. The flaws have to be yours, because you're the one projecting them.

If you say that you love your husband, what does that have to do with him? You're just telling him who you are. You tell the story of how he's handsome and fascinating and sexy, and you love your story about him. You're projecting that he's your story. And then when he doesn't give you what you want, you may tell the story of how he's mean, he's controlling, he's selfish—and what does *that* have to do with him?

If my husband says, "I adore you," I think, *Good. I love that he thinks I'm his sweet dream. How happy he must feel about that!* If he were ever to come to me and say, "The sorriest day of my life was when I married you," still, what would that have to do with me? He'd just be in a sad dream this time, and I might think, *Oh, poor baby, he's having a nightmare. I hope he wakes up soon.* It's not personal. How can it have anything to do with me? I love him, and if what he says about me isn't true in my experience, I'll ask him if there's anything I can do for him. If I can do it, I will, and if it's not honest for me, I won't. He is left with his story.

You're living with God disguised as your husband, and he will show you all your unclear places; he will give you everything you need in order to get free. That's love. When you see your partner as God, your Work becomes very simple.

All love songs make sense if we remember what it is that we truly love. If the "you" of a song is another person, then the song is a lie. It has to be, because we can never find our completion in another person. It always comes back to us. So when we put God in the "you" of these songs, we see how true they all are. Every love song is written for God by God.

When you keep manipulating your partner to get her to love you, everything you do has that motive, even when you take her out to dinner. It's very painful. Awareness is a wonderful thing, and look forward to manipulating her again, because when you step into inquiry, your patterns change, and you become a total question mark. It's incredibly exciting that you don't even know who you are aside from your motives. And once you begin doing The Work, you can take her out to dinner and you're unlimited. Or you can not take her out to dinner and you're unlimited. That's how it is. You love yourself totally, and she doesn't have to participate, so there is no motive in "I love you." Without a motive, the pain disappears. Your thinking about what she was thinking about you was your hell. You had to puff yourself up to match all your beliefs about what you thought she was thinking; you had to be the Marlboro man. And when she had sex with you, you saw that as validation that your delusion was right.

If my husband were to say, "Stay home with me, I don't want you to be with people," and if I knew to be with people, I would say, "Thank you, sweetheart, I understand where you're coming from. And I'm going to be with people now." I've met him with some understanding. His is equal to mine. And I'm going to be with people now. I would tell him what I call the whole truth and nothing but the truth. "I need to be with people now" is just part of it. The rest of it is "I love you." "I love you, and I'm going to be with people now." But if I needed something from him, if I wanted his approval, that would be another story. So I turn it around—I want *my* approval. And if I sold out for approval, it wouldn't feel honest inside me; there would be no peace. I'd be treating my husband as not my nature if I were to seek his approval or love. It's unkind. And if I'm unkind to him, I'm unkind to me.

Once you open to love, you lose your whole world. It's over. Love leaves nothing. It's totally greedy. Our pain is in denying it. A boundary is an act of selfishness. There is nothing you wouldn't give to anyone if you weren't afraid. And you can't do that ahead of your time. You don't have to give anything, for now; just investigate your thinking, do The Work. When you meet your thoughts with understanding, you discover that there's nothing to lose. So eventually there's no attempt at protection. Then giving everything you have becomes a privilege.

To exclude anything that appears in your universe is not love. Love joins with everything. It doesn't exclude the monster. It doesn't avoid the nightmare—it looks forward to it.

If I want love, I can't have it. I *am* love, and as long as I seek it from you, I can't know that. To love you is to separate. I *am* love, and that is as close as it can get.

Love says, "I love you no matter what." Love says, "You're fine the way you are." And that is the only thing that can heal; that is the only way you can join. If you think he's supposed to be different from what he is, you don't love him. In that moment you love who he's going to be when you're through manipulating him. He is a throwaway until he matches your image of him.

You can't disappoint another human being. And another human being can't disappoint you. You believe the story of how your partner isn't giving you what you want, and you disappoint yourself. If you want something from your partner and he says no, that's reality. It leaves *you*. And you can always give it to yourself.

You're just suffering from the belief that there's something missing from your life. In reality, you always have what you need.

People think that relationships will make them happy, but you can't get happiness from the other person or from anywhere outside you. A relationship is two belief systems that come together to validate that there's something outside you that can bring you happiness. And when you think that that's true, growing beyond your common belief system means losing the other person, because that's what you had together. So if you move forward, you leave this old belief system behind in what you call the other person, and then you feel it as separation and pain.

We are love, and there's nothing we can do about that. Love is our nature. It's what we are without our stories.

For the personality, love is nothing more than agreement. If I agree with you, you love me. And the minute I don't agree with you, the minute I question one of your sacred beliefs, I become your enemy; you divorce me in your mind. Then you start looking for all the reasons why you're right, and you stay focused outside yourself. When you're focused outside and believe that your problem is caused by someone else, rather than by your attachment to the story you're believing in the moment, then you are your own victim, and the situation appears to be hopeless.

You can't love anyone; you only love your story about them.

There's a story I like to tell about Roxann, my daughter. She called me one day and said she wanted me to attend my grandson's birthday party. I told her I had a commitment that day, I was going to do a public event in another city. She was so hurt and angry that she hung up on me. Then, maybe ten minutes later, she called me back and said, "I'm so excited, Momma. I just did The Work on you, and I saw that there is

nothing you can do to keep me from loving you."
That is what we all have with the technology of this
Work. There is nothing you can do to keep someone
from loving you. And there is nothing anyone can
ever do to keep you from loving them. It's not personal. It's about who you are.

Anytime you find yourself wanting sympathy, you're
trying to get someone to join you in your mythology.
And it always hurts.

A relationship is two people who agree, two people
who like each other's stories. We call it "love." And
when our partner doesn't agree with our sacred story,
the one we will stake our identity on, we divorce him.
If someone says I'm unkind, I run to my husband
and say, "Honey, so-and-so says I'm unkind." And
he hugs me and strokes my cheek and says, "Well,
that's just not true. Of course you're kind!" That way,
I don't have to go inside and know the truth of the
criticism for myself. I get my ally to fight on my side,
and I call his agreement "love." If I go home and say,
"Sweetheart, so-and-so says I'm unkind," and he says,

"Well, you know, sometimes you *are* unkind, and here's how," and if I would rather have him agree with me than tell the truth, I'll feel hurt and angry, and then I'll go out and find a friend who *will* agree with me. Maybe that will work! But sooner or later it becomes too painful. So I have to stop and go inside and set myself free. My husband can't give me that. Only I can.

When you believe the thought that anyone should love you, that's where the pain begins. I often say, "If I had a prayer, it would be: 'God spare me from the desire for love, approval, or appreciation. Amen.'" To seek people's love and approval assumes that you aren't whole.

The only relationship that is ever going to be meaningful is the relationship you have with yourself. When you love yourself, you love the person you're always with. But unless you love yourself, you won't be comfortable with someone else, because they're going to challenge your belief system, and until you inquire, you've got to do war to defend it. So much for relationship. People make these unspoken contracts with each other and promise each other that they won't ever mess with the other person's belief system, and of course, that's not possible.

How do you react when you think you need people's love? Do you become a slave for their approval? Do you live an inauthentic life because you can't bear the thought that they might disapprove of you? Do you try to figure out how they would like you to be, and then try to become that, like a chameleon?

In fact, you never really get their love. You turn into someone you aren't, and then when they say "I love you," you can't believe it, because they're loving a façade. They're loving someone who doesn't even exist, the person you're pretending to be. It's difficult to seek other people's love. It's deadly. In seeking it, you lose what is genuine. This is the prison we create for ourselves as we seek what we already have.

Romantic love is the story of how you need another person to complete you. It's an absolutely insane story. My experience is that I don't need anyone to complete me. As soon as I realize that, everyone completes me.

Hurt feelings or discomfort of any kind cannot be caused by another person. No one outside me can hurt me. That's not a possibility. It's only when I believe a story that I get hurt. And I'm the one who's hurting me by believing what I think. This is very good news, because it means that I don't have to get someone else to stop hurting me. I'm the one who can stop hurting me. It's within my power.

Everything is equal. There is no this person or that person. There's only One. And that's the last story. It doesn't matter how you attempt to be disconnected; it's not a possibility. The thought that you're believing is an attempt to break the connection. But it's only an attempt. It can't be done. That's why it feels so uncomfortable. It's an attempt to identify as an "I." And that's a full-time job, until it's not.

21

Only you can kick yourself out of paradise. So if you are Adam and you look to Eve for completion, you have just kicked yourself out of paradise. You could just experience your own nature, which is to love yourself, and therefore her, with no separation. But if you want something from her, if you think you need her love or approval, you suffer. There's only one way I can use you to complete me, and that is if I judge you, inquire, and turn it around.

The worst loss you've ever experienced is the greatest gift you can have.

Who would you be in people's presence without the story that anyone should care about you, ever? You would be love itself. When you believe this myth that people should care, you lose caring about people and about yourself. Love can't come from "out there"; it can only come from inside you. The way that I know that is because it does.

I was once walking in the desert with a man who began to have a stroke. We sat down, and he said, "Oh, my God, I'm dying, do something." I just sat there beside him, loving him, looking into his eyes, knowing that we were miles from a phone or car. He said, "You don't even care, do you?" I said, "No." He was talking through one side of his mouth because the other side had become paralyzed, and when I said no, he started to laugh, and I did, too. And then his faculties returned. The stroke came to pass, not to stay. This is the power of love. I wouldn't leave him for a caring.

You've never reacted to someone else. You project meaning onto nothing. There's nothing separate out there. And you react to the meaning you've projected. Loneliness comes from an honest place—you're the only one here. There are no humans here. You're it. This world doesn't even exist. When you investigate your thoughts and stop believing your projections, you come to realize that. It's the end of the world. The end of a world that never existed anyway.

I am always what I judge you to be in the moment. There's no exception. I am my own pain. I am my own happiness.

As long as you believe any concept, you're going to impose it onto your husband, your wife, your lover, your children. Sooner or later, when you don't get what you want from them or when they threaten what you think you have, you're going to impose this concept onto them, until you meet it with some understanding. This is not a guess—this is what we do. We're not attached to people; we're attached to concepts.

Nothing can cost you someone you love. The only thing that can cost you your husband is if you believe a thought. That's how you move away from him. That's how the marriage ends. You are one with your husband until you believe the thought that he should look a certain way, he should give you something, or he should be something other than what he is. That's how you divorce him. Right then and there you have lost your marriage.

Have you noticed how you get really happy when your partner does what you want? So you have to become a controller to put him in a position where he always does what you want. I say, be grateful when he does what you want; and when he doesn't, skip the middleman and do it yourself.

Until you are loyal to yourself, you can't be loyal to another person.

Defense is the first act of war. If you tell me that I'm mean, rejecting, hard, unkind, or unfair, I say, "Thank you, sweetheart, I can find all these in my life, I have been everything you say, and more. Tell me everything you see, and together we can help me understand. Through you, I come to know myself. Without you, how can I know the places in me that are unkind and invisible? You bring me to myself. So, sweetheart, look into my eyes and tell me again. I want you to give me everything."

This is how friends meet. It's called integrity. I am all things. If you see me as unkind, that is an opportunity for me to go inside and look at what appears in my life. Have I ever been unkind? I can find it. Have I ever acted unfairly? That doesn't take me long to acknowledge. If I'm a bit cloudy about it, my children can fill me in. What could anyone call me that I couldn't find at some time in my life? If you say one single thing that I have the urge to defend, that thing is the very pearl waiting inside me to be discovered.

No one can leave you—only you can do that. Whatever your partner's commitment is, your commitment is what you can count on, until it changes. A long-term commitment is for this very moment. Even if he says he is committed to you forever, you can never know that, because as long as you believe that there is a "you" and a "him," it's only a personality committing to a personality; and personalities don't love, they want something.

Until you can be happy that he's gone, for *his* sake (which is for your sake), your Work is not done. So it's good that your thoughts wake you up in the middle of the night curled up in a ball of terror. Do

The Work on these projections that are so powerful. You are your own freedom. Look at how you've lived with him, what you have done to make sure that he thought you were "the one." You've lost your life; you think you have no life without him. It's good that he leaves you, so that you can come to know who you really are.

I once spoke with a man who had been doing The Work for a while. His wife fell in love with another man, and instead of going into sadness and panic, he questioned his thinking. "'She should stay with me'—is it true? I can't know that. How do I react when I believe the thought? Extremely upset. Who would I be without the thought? I would love her and just want the best for her." This man really wanted to know the truth. When he questioned his thinking, he found something extremely precious.

"Eventually," he said, "I was able to see it as something that *should* be happening, because it was. And I was able to say to my wife, 'Tell me everything about it, as if I were your best girlfriend.' She didn't have to censor any of it to protect me. It was amazing to hear about her experience. I felt so much joy for her. It was the most liberating experience I've ever had."

His wife moved in with the other man, and he was fine with that, because he didn't want her to stay if she didn't want to. A few months later, she hit a crisis point with her new lover and needed someone to talk to. She went to her best friend—her husband. They calmly discussed her options. He really loved her and just hoped she'd be clear about what she wanted. She decided to get a place of her own where she could work things out, and eventually she went back to their marriage.

Through all this, whenever the man found himself mentally at war with what was happening and experienced pain or fear, he inquired into the thought he was believing at that moment and returned to a calm and cheerful state of mind. He came to know for himself that the only possible problem he could have was his own uninvestigated thinking. His wife gave him everything he needed for his own freedom.

A commitment is your truth, and there's no higher and no lower. You are committing yourself to your own truth. "I love, honor, and obey you; and I may change my mind." That's as good as it gets. I'm married only to God—reality. That's where my commitment is, for better or for worse. It can't be to a particular person.

And my husband wouldn't want it any other way. So unless we marry the truth, there's no real marriage.

How would you function if you didn't have your pain and unhappiness? I'm asking you to seriously go inside. How would it be if you smiled all the time, if you were free all the time? It would mean that you wouldn't have control and couldn't manipulate people—that insane idea wouldn't even occur to you. This is how you manipulate: "You should be with me," "If you leave, I'll be miserable." You use these thoughts to get us to agree with your story that there is misery in this world, though the truth is that in your essence you are love, whether you like it or not. You can know that because if you're one thought away from love, you hurt.

We marry ourselves or there is no marriage. That is the only love affair that's real. I am married within myself, I love myself, and that's what I project onto everyone. I am a lover of what is, and I don't want anything else. I only know I want to be here with you now. I *am* here with you—that's how I know that I want to be. It wasn't planned; it's simply unfolding. I love you completely, and you don't even have to participate, so there's no motive in "I love you." Isn't that fine! I can love you completely and you have nothing to do with it. There is nothing you can do to keep me from the intimacy I experience with you. When you have a stressful belief about your partner, you have separated from yourself, divorced yourself, and therefore you have divorced him, and it hurts. When you move away from yourself to your partner, you have divorced yourself.

So when we have no beliefs about how reality should look, we're truly married, and it doesn't hurt. It's internal. There is no relationship outside that.

I can't feel your pain. That's not possible. If someone hits you and I believe that I "feel" it, I am projecting what that must feel like, and *that* is the pain I feel. I'm remembering the time when someone hit me, and I feel my own story. In reality, there's no pain for me. There aren't two of us in pain; there's only one. Who would I be without my story? Pain-free, happy, and totally available if someone needs me.

I hear people say that compassion means feeling someone else's pain, as if that were even possible. And how are you most present, most available—when you're in pain or when you're clear and happy? When someone is hurting, why would they want you to be hurting, too? Wouldn't they rather have you totally present and available?

How can you be present for people if you believe that you're feeling their pain? If a car runs over someone and you're in terror, projecting what it must feel like, you become paralyzed. But sometimes in a crisis like that, the mind loses its reference, it can't project anymore, you don't think, you just act, you run over and pick up the car before you have time to feel or plan or think, *This isn't possible.* It happens in a split second. Who would you be without your story? The car is up in the air.

"If you loved someone with all your heart, you would be sexual"—can you absolutely know that that's true? What happens when you believe the thought that you can't get too close to a man or you'll be sexual?

How does it feel when you think you have to hold yourself back from love? Who would you be without the story "I would be sexual if I fell into his arms"? You would be you, naturally. It's a very painful thing, the fear of oneself. Through the power of inquiry, you come to realize for yourself that you are love. There's nothing you can do about it.

A commitment is my truth in the moment. And if I want commitment, I'm going to find it only inside myself right now. If I want someone else to be committed to me or if I want to be committed to someone else, it's hopeless, because it's personality committing to personality; and as I often say, personalities don't love, they want something. When I commit to something, I follow it through, and I reserve the right to change my mind.

Commitment is a wonderful path. It happens one moment at a time. I promise in one moment, and then in another moment I may change my mind. I keep my word until I don't. And people tell me that in their experience I do keep my commitments. If someone says that I didn't, I say, "Isn't that interesting! I changed my mind, or really, *it* changed. I'm not doing it; it's doing me. I can see that you really believe that I should have kept my commitment. It changed. And, if we wait, it could change back." And it could. I'm not doing it.

How do you know that you don't need a romantic partner? You don't have one. How do you know that you need one? Here he is! You don't call the shots on this. It's better that you don't. That way you can give yourself everything. What do you need a partner for? To fill your hunger? Is that true? All your adult life you've thought that you needed a partner, and you're still hungry. So how many partners does it take to fill you? I'm not saying that you don't need a partner. This is about your own truth. Just go in and experience it. Need *yourself*, whether or not you find a partner. In the meantime, you are waiting just for you.

Do you want to meet the love of your life? Look in the mirror.

How do you treat your husband when you want him to love you? Can you see a stress-free reason to want him to love you, or to want anyone on this planet to love you? If I have the thought that I want my husband to love me, it's not love. I want him to love whomever he loves. I may as well, because that's what he does anyway. I know I can't redirect it; I'm not a fool anymore. And people call that love, but I'm just a lover of what is. I know the joy of loving, so I know it's not my business how he directs his love. My business is to love him.

Have you noticed how many times you try to control what comes in by giving rather than receiving? What happens when you just stand there and receive? The receiving *is* the giving. It's the most genuine thing you can give back. When someone comes to hug me, I don't have to hug them back. To receive it—you can die in that! To receive it is to die to pain, and to be born into love and laughter.

I was privileged to be married to someone who had zero interest in inquiry. And if I had believed that he needed The Work, *I* would have needed The Work. If I had believed that he needed to trust me, *I* would have needed to trust *him*. And I did trust him. I trusted him to do exactly what he did. So there was nowhere I could go but a perfect marriage. If I hadn't loved him with all my heart, I would have been insane. It had nothing to do with him. And that didn't mean I had to live with him.

The thing you're terrified of losing—you've already lost it. You may not have noticed that yet, and it may take you a while to grieve, and then you may realize that there was never anything to lose.

To believe the story that someone has left you is to leave yourself. That's how you divorce yourself. Every time you're in your partner's business, dictating whom he should be with, whom he should or shouldn't leave, you have left yourself, and the effect of that is loneliness and terror. Until you question what you believe, you remain the innocent cause of your own suffering.

The voice within is what I'm married to. All marriage is a metaphor for that marriage. My lover is the place that an honest yes or no comes from. That's my true partner. It's always there. And to tell you yes when my integrity says no is to divorce that partner.

No one who says "I should love myself" knows what love is. Love is what we are already. So to think that you should love yourself when you don't is pure delusion. Isn't the turnaround truer? "I shouldn't love myself." How do you know that you shouldn't love yourself? You don't! That's it, for now. The truth is no respecter of spiritual concepts. "I should love myself"—ugh, on what planet? Love is not a doing. There is nothing you have to do. And when you question your mind, you can see that the only thing that keeps you from being love is a stressful thought.

When you know who you are, there is no one you can't get along with. It takes only one, and that one is you. You can go downtown and pick a perfect stranger and get married and have a happy life. You're always with the perfect mate.

I don't want people's approval. I want people to think the way they think. That's love. Manipulating and trying to change someone is like trying to rape his mind. "You there! Stop your internal life and focus over here, on me! I absolutely know that it's in your best interest to approve of me. I want that, and I don't care what you want." But you can't control someone else's thinking. You can't even control your own. There's no one thinking anyway. It's a house of mirrors. Seeking approval means being stuck in the thought "I'm a this," this little speck, this limited thing.

Marry yourself and you have married us. We are you. That's the cosmic joke.

If my husband asks, "Would you please bring me a cup of tea?" I know what my joy is—he just told me.

That's how I know what to do. I know what it feels like when he brings me a cup of tea, the joy and gratitude that simple act gives me. The belief that he should get it for himself, or that he's using me, or that it's not my turn—that's what hurts. There is no belief that can stand up to inquiry, no genuine inquiry that can leave me as anything but love. Me serving me. To give him anything he wants is to give it to myself.

The reality is that without a story you're genderless—not male, not female, not even human. You're not anything. *It* is not anything, it's more than that. It's all-inclusive; it doesn't even question. There are no questions in the void; there is only the experience of it. And not even that.

We use our beauty, our cleverness, our charm, to capture someone for a partnership, as if he were an animal. And then when he wants to get out of the cage, we're furious. That doesn't sound very caring to me. It's not self-love. I want my husband to want what he wants. And I also notice that I don't have a choice. That's self-love. He does what he does, and

I love that. That's what I want, because when I'm at war with reality, it hurts.

There's a lot to be said for monogamy. It's the ultimate symbol for One, because it keeps your mind focused on one primary person. You just have to undo everything around him, every story about him that rises up in your mind. Monogamy is a sacred thing, because the mind can be very still in that position.

One person will give you the experience that a million people could give you. There's only one mind. Your partner will bring up every concept ever known to humanity, in every combination, so that you can come to know yourself. If you can just learn to love the one you're with, you have met self-love.

If you don't attach beliefs to it, sex is just like breathing or walking. It's beauty; it's you. But when you go into it seeking things like satisfaction, ecstasy, intimacy, connectedness, and romance, don't count on finding them.

"An erection means that you're sexually aroused"—is that true? Are you sure? Do you believe everything you think? What does it really mean? It's an erection. That's it. The story you tell about it is where your suffering begins. For example, if you have the belief that you should put your erection somewhere, and there is nowhere to put it, that's what is hurting you. If you didn't believe the thought that you should do something with it, you would simply join with it, you'd become it, and it would be a complete experience—the beginning, the middle, and the end. No climax, no ejaculation, just a beautiful erect penis, coming from nowhere and with nowhere to go.

Your partner has nothing to do with your experience of making love—nothing. You touch him and you tell the story of what that means. He touches you and you tell the story of what that means, and you turn yourself on, or you turn yourself off. If you believe the thought that he's touching you in the wrong way, you turn yourself off. You think you know something. The truth is that it's God making love with God, and there are no rules. And if you want to participate, be fully present. Your partner is not supposed to participate, he is just your story: "He's doing it right," "He's doing it wrong," "He's thinking this," "He's thinking that," "If he really loved me, he would . . ." On and on, and it's nothing but your story.

Without your story, have you ever really experienced sex? Never. No one ever has. We all have a story about what sex is. You're trying to get it to match your story about it: It's good, it's bad, you're a good lover, you're not, he should do this, he should do that. You're always trying to live up to your own story. What happens through sex is that you have beliefs about who he is, who you are, what your touch means, what his touch means, what this sensation means, what that emotion means. You tell yourself a story about all of it, and you call it good or bad. Who would you be without your story? You'd be free. To not know is my favorite part. And the truth is, you *don't* know. Without your story, you would have sex and love it, or not have sex and love it. It would just be what it is.

No one is mentally ill, no one is frigid: these are just terms we use to separate ourselves, to stay lost. You tell the story of who men are and what sex is, and you freeze yourself up. You're not frigid; you're attached to an unquestioned story. Question your beliefs and who knows what kind of lover you'll be? It has nothing to do with sexual pleasure. When you meet your thoughts with understanding, you meet yourself. You become your own lover. Ultimately, that's whom you're sleeping with.

If my husband were to have an affair and that were not okay with me, I would say, "Sweetheart, I understand that you're having an affair, and I notice that when you do that, something inside me tends to move away from you. I don't know what that is, I only know that it's so; it mirrors your movement away from me, and I want you to know that." And then if he were to continue his affair, to prefer to spend his time with another woman, I might notice that I was moving away, but I wouldn't have to leave him in anger.

There's nothing I can do to stay with him, and there's nothing I can do to divorce him. I'm not running this show. I might stay with him, or I might divorce him in a state of total love, and think, *This is fascinating; we promised we would be together always, and I'm divorcing him now,* and I would probably

42

laugh, love that he has what he wants, and move on, because there is no war in me. And someone else would divorce her husband, thinking, *He shouldn't have had the affair, he hurt me, he doesn't deserve me, he broke his promises, he's heartless.* Either way, the movement is the same; the only difference is the story.

You're going to make the trip either way. The question is, *how* are you going to do it? Are you going to go kicking and screaming; or are you going to go with dignity, generosity, and peace? You can't dictate this, you can't fake it, and you can't make yourself be spiritual or loving. Just be honest and question your thinking. Then, eventually, when people say, "Oh, it's a terrible thing, this divorce," you might respond, "I understand how you see it that way, and that's not my experience at all."

Love wouldn't deny a breath. It wouldn't deny a grain of sand or a speck of dust. It is totally in love with itself; and it delights in acknowledging itself through its own presence, in every way, without limit. It embraces it all, everything from the murderer and the rapist to the saint to the dog and cat. Love is so vast within itself that it will burn you up. It's so vast that there's nothing you can do with it. All you can do is *be* it.

The difference between pleasure and joy? Ohh . . . the distance is from here to the moon! From here to another galaxy! Pleasure is an attempt to fill yourself. Joy is what you are.

There is no way to join your partner except to get free of your belief that you want something from him, and then to give yourself to him totally. That's true joining. Our nature is to give, but we get confused about what it is that we're to give. The truth that you experience is how I join with you; that's how you touch me, and you touch me so intimately that it brings me to tears. I don't know what it is that you're doing, but I have joined you, and you don't have a choice. And I can do this over and over and over, endlessly, effortlessly. It's called making love.

When you come to the place where you don't want anything from your partner, it's like "Bingo! You just won the lottery!" If I want something from my partner, I need to take a look at my thinking. I already have everything. We all do. That's how I can sit here so comfortably: I don't want anything from you. I don't even want your freedom, if you don't. I don't even want your peace. But if you want it, that's all that's left of my want. So I'm going to join you there, because I remember what it was to want. And if you're not interested in your freedom, then that's what I want. I want your heaven, I want your hell, I want whatever you want, because I love you.

ON HEALTH,
SICKNESS, AND DEATH

Every story is about body-identification. Without a story, there's no body.

Bodies don't think, care, or have any problem with themselves. They never beat themselves up or shame themselves. They simply try to keep themselves balanced and healthy. They're entirely efficient, intelligent, kind, and resourceful. Where there's no thought, there's no problem. It's the story we believe—prior to doing inquiry—that leaves us confused. I tell the story of my body, and because I haven't inquired, I believe that my body is the problem and that if only this or that changed, I'd be happy. But my suffering can't be my body's fault.

Your body is not your business. If you need a doctor, go to one. That way, you get to be free. Your body is your doctor's business. *Your* business is your thinking; and in the peace of that, you're very clear about what to do. And then the body becomes a lot of fun, because you're not invested in whether it lives or dies. It's nothing more than a metaphor for your thinking, mirrored back to you.

If I lose all my money, good. If I get cancer, good. If my husband leaves me, good. If he stays, that's good, too. Who wouldn't always say yes to reality if that's what you're in love with? What can happen that I wouldn't welcome with all my heart?

I don't change, and I only see change in you if you say that there's change. You are my inner life. You're the voice of my self, reporting my health at all times.

Sickness or health—it's all fine with me. You're sad, you're not sad; you don't understand, you understand; you're peaceful, you're upset; you're this, you're that. I am each cell reporting itself. And beyond all change, I know that each cell is always at peace.

For people who are tired of the pain, nothing could be worse than trying to control what can't be controlled. If you want real control, drop the illusion of control; let life have you. It does anyway. You're just telling the story about how it doesn't. That story can never be real. You didn't make the weather or the sun or the moon. You have no control over your lungs or your heart or your ability to see or walk. One minute you're fine and healthy, and the next minute you're not. When we try to be safe, we live our lives being very, very careful; and we wind up having no lives. I like to say, "Don't be careful; you could hurt yourself."

Bodies don't crave, bodies don't want, bodies don't know, don't care, don't get hungry or thirsty. It's what that mind attaches to—ice cream, alcohol, drugs, sex, money—that the body reflects. There are no physical addictions, only mental ones. Body follows mind. It doesn't have a choice. Actually, it's simultaneous, but as long as you're mentally experiencing duality, body follows mind.

What fun is it to be God if I can't get a glimpse of myself in the mirror? And whether I like it or not, that's what I am. I'm vanity—total vanity. So when people are attached to their looks and their health, it's coming from an honest source. It's just misinterpreted. It's pure innocence.

All the thoughts we attach to are about survival, then health, then comfort, then pleasure. Every thought has to be about "I"; that's how you survive. And then as soon as you get your little house, your little car, your little piece of turf, your thoughts turn to the story of how you need to be healthy and comfortable. You put stuff in the shopping cart, you put stuff in the house, and as soon as you're comfortable, your thoughts turn to pleasure. This is full-scale body-identification: there's no thought that isn't about the body. So you go to pleasure when you have your little ducks in order. And all pleasure is pain, because you're worried about losing it, and trying to make it last or to get more of it. You never really experience it; you're always in its past or future.

I once did The Work with a woman who was ashamed of her fingers. She had developed rheumatoid arthritis when she was seventeen, and she believed that her fingers were deformed. They weren't normal, she thought, and she suffered a lot from that belief; she was embarrassed even to let people see them. But her fingers *were* normal: they were normal for *her*. They were the fingers she had woken up with every morning since she was seventeen. For twenty-seven years they were her normal fingers. She just hadn't noticed.

How do you react when you believe that what is isn't normal for you? Shame, sadness, despair. Who would you be without that thought? At ease with your condition and loving it, whatever it is, because you would realize that it is completely normal, for you. Even if 99 percent of other people look a different way, their normal isn't your normal: *this* is your normal. That dear woman's argument with reality was what caused her suffering, not her fingers.

Give us permission, through you, to have a flaw, because flaws are the norm. When you hide your flaws, you teach us to do that. I love to say that we're just waiting for one teacher, just one, to give us permission to be who we are now, so that we can all come to know that that's what is normal for us. You appear as this now. That's such a gift to give. The pain is in withholding it. Who else is going to give us permission to be free, if not you? Do it for your own sake, and we'll follow. We're a reflection of your thinking, and when you free yourself, we all get free.

It's not ever going to be about food or alcohol or drugs or money or health. We just keep using symbols to stay body-identified. And eventually nothing holds.

You're in the perfect health, whether you like it or not. You tell the story of how you're supposed to be stronger or healthier so that you don't have to know that your condition is perfect. My condition is perfect for what I need to do now, for where I need to be now. I'm without a future.

The body is never our problem. Our problem is always a thought that we innocently believe. The Work deals with our thinking, not with the object that we think we're addicted to. There *is* no such thing as an addiction to an object; there is only an attachment to the uninvestigated concept arising in the moment.

When we're sick, we want people to be kind to us. And yet we're not being kind to ourselves, because we're lying in bed with an enemy: our disease. Until we're at peace with our worst enemy, which always is our thinking, we can't love our beloved partner or our precious child. Sooner or later, everything we think about our disease will have to be attached to our partner or our child when we don't get our way or when we think we're going to lose something.

We don't resist our diseases; we resist our thoughts about them. Without our story, we can't have a problem. We can only have a solution.

Bodies are as innocent as trees or flowers or breath.

There's nothing else to do but get well, and that's not up to the body. Ultimately the body isn't going to make it. This is good news—it's over, forget it, let's work with what we do have. Can you get it from here? If this body story were true, it would mean that no fat person could be self-realized, no one in a wheelchair, no one old or sick, no one who isn't beautiful. This leaves out practically the whole human race! Almost no one has a chance for freedom under this theory. We're all waiting until we get the body perfect to be peaceful. Can we just do it from here, now?

If it comes to me to take my estrogen, I do it. If it doesn't come to me, I don't. So I'm always directed. And they say, "Oh, poor thing, she died because she didn't take her whatever-it-was." Well, *you're* stuck with that story, and I'm free. And so are you if you do inquiry, because it's always about the story. That's why it's so wonderful to be sick and to get old. It's wonderful to lose your legs or your arms or your eyes or your loved ones. Investigate the stressful thoughts you have about your condition until you see that it's the perfect condition for you.

When you believe your thoughts, you rape your body by saying that it should be more beautiful, it should be healthier, it should be taller, shorter, fatter, thinner, younger, stronger. You take a perfect body and trash it.

Awareness is so much more exciting than a body.

My heart is always healthy. Even if it were having an attack, it would be healthy. It's perfect for that moment. Whether it's beating strongly or blasting into oblivion, it's as it should be. If you argue with what's happening, you'll have a heart attack with a lot of fear. But without a story, without arguing with reality, you can have a heart attack in peace. "Wow! So this is how she goes out, so this is how the story ends!" A heart attack can be very exciting. This is just about awareness. The awareness of what is: you are that movement itself. (And not even that.)

When you're asleep, does your body hurt? When you're in the worst pain and the phone rings and it's the call you've been waiting for and you're mentally focused on the phone call, there's no pain. If you change your thinking, you change the pain.

I was in Holland a few years ago, and I was running a very high fever. And The Work went on every day. I was working with people from early morning until late at night. And I noticed that a few times during a break, I would be just huddled up in a corner, exhausted, with a high fever, in heaven. My body is not my business. If you don't tell me I'm sick, I have no way of knowing. And in the clarity of that, I always seem to be well. No story: no sickness. There was snow, there was cold, there was sky, there were people, there was breath, there was fever, there was exhaustion, there was joy—everything! Without a story, I'm free.

How do you live when you believe that your health problems shouldn't be there? You can't even tell us the truth. You can't even cough or blow your nose honestly, or let us know you're not feeling well. Who would you be without the story "I should feel better"? You'd be free.

I love this old-age thing. It blows apart every concept about health. "I'm ninety years old and I have arthritis, but I should move fluidly." I don't think so! That kind of thinking is true masochism. When I say that my body should move fluidly, how does that make me feel when it doesn't?

There's no "vibration" that's higher or lower or different. There's only a story that would separate them out. All together there's one vibration. You vibrationally match everything you've got in the moment. And you have everything, so you're a perfect match. "If you had a higher vibration, you'd have better health"—can you absolutely know that that's true?

How do you live when you believe that your vibrations are too low to heal your body? Masochism. War. Who would you be without that theory? A little more relaxed, a little more ready for healing.

Bodies don't have the power to take away your peace. I'd rather be happy instead and let the body do what it does.

When you believe that you are this body, you stay limited, small, apparently encapsulated as one separate form. So every thought has to be about your survival or your comfort or your pleasure, because if you let up for a moment, there would be no body-identification. When you dream, you are the whole dream and everything in it. You have to be: you're the dreamer. You're bodiless, you're free—you're a man, you're a woman, a dog, a tree, you're all of it simultaneously; you're in the kitchen one moment and on a mountaintop the next; you're in New York and suddenly you're in Hawaii; nothing is ever stable because you can't body-identify; there's no identification you can attach to. That's how unlimited the mind is when there's no particular body to be.

Someone said this morning, "You look like you're losing weight." Good. "You look like you're gaining weight." Good. "You look old." Good. "You look young." Good. Body is not my business. My thinking is. So watch the masochistic thoughts you believe in order to stay body-identified. And have fun!

A peaceful mind doesn't care about a body.

"Your shoulder shouldn't hurt"—is that true? It hurts exactly the way it does. It *should* hurt exactly the way it does. It's a flat-out lie that it shouldn't. Your story is how you keep yourself in time and space and duality. This is not a right or wrong. We're looking at reality here.

If you argue with reality, if you lie about what you know is true, it feels stressful. It opposes what you are. "It's not supposed to hurt like this": Feel how painful that thought is. How many times have you been there? I used to live in that place. I lived there, in bed, for years. No wonder you cry when you say, "My shoulder shouldn't hurt this much," because your shoulder *should* hurt this much. It should because it does. That's reality.

Every belief is about being careful; it's about keeping the body alive. I'm not careful. I don't live that way. I look forward to whatever comes.

If you believe that certain foods are really good for you, and you love eating those foods, and you feel good when you eat them, and it feels like loving yourself, that sounds very sweet to me. It sounds like a peaceful, honest way of living. The war starts when you believe that other people should eat that way too: your partner or your children, for example. You can't know what's best for them. Maybe your carrot is their ice cream. You just can't know their path. Do you know yours?

I once went for twenty-seven days without food. There was no reason for it—I just knew not to eat.

And during all those days I couldn't find a trace of hunger. Hunger was just another myth. My family and friends were fearful for my life, but I wasn't concerned; I felt healthy and strong. The whole time, I was doing a lot of vigorous walking in the desert. And at no moment did I experience anything but myths about hunger and bellyaches and weight loss. I couldn't find one legitimate need that didn't come face-to-face with the fear of death. And then, after twenty-seven days, for no reason, I ate.

There's no suffering in the world; there's only a story that would lead you to believe it. There's no suffering in the world that's real. Isn't that amazing? Investigate and come to know it for yourself.

Pain is a friend. It's nothing I want to get rid of, if I can't. I'm a lover of what is. It's a sweet visitor; it can stay as long as it wants to. (And this doesn't mean that I won't take the Tylenol.)

"Yoga makes your shoulder feel better"—that's one of your sacred beliefs. Can you really know that that's why your shoulder stopped hurting? When you're focused on your shoulder, focused on "yoga (or massage or carrot juice) is going to make it better," you're body-identified. At night we pass out from these concepts. We don't sleep, we pass out. You're scared of pain in your body. When the carrot juice stops working, you're left with your own thought system. You try to hold it off with yoga.

There's only one true yoga, and it's mental, and it's a free flow. I'm a lover of what is. I have tested all these theories, and I know that even if the massage or the yoga or the carrot juice or the wheat grass work now, eventually I'll have the grace of getting old and knowing that they can't help. Or hopefully I'll get some kind of disease, where all this thought catches up with me, and I can take a look at my stressful concepts. It's all grace.

And don't you want it all? Freedom from the body, freedom from the concept that you are a body. Something's always going to hurt. Ultimately you're left with your thinking about your body. That's all there is to work with.

If you think that alcohol makes you sick or confused or angry, then when you drink it it's as if you're drinking your own disease. You're meeting alcohol where it is, and it does exactly what you know it will do. So investigate the thinking, not in order to stop drinking, but simply to end any confusion about what alcohol will do. And if you believe that you really want to keep drinking, just notice what it does to you. There's no pity in it. There's no victim in it. And eventually there's no fun in it—only a hangover.

I suggest that you not do The Work with the motive of healing your body. Go in for the love of truth. Heal your mind. Meet your concepts with understanding. I love to say that when you finally get your body totally healthy, it may get hit by a truck. So can we be happy right here, not tomorrow, not in ten minutes—can we be happy right now? I use the word *happy* to mean in a natural state of peace and clarity, and that's what The Work gives us.

Even physical pain isn't real; it's the story of a past, always leaving, never arriving. But people don't know that. My grandson Racey fell down once when he was three years old. He scraped his knee, and there was some blood, and he began to cry. And as he looked up at me, I said, "Sweetheart, are you remembering when you fell down and hurt yourself?" And immediately the crying stopped. That was it. He must have realized, for a moment, that pain is always in the past. The moment of pain is always gone. It's a remembering of what we think is true, and it projects what no longer exists. (I'm not saying that your pain isn't real for you. I know pain, and it hurts! That's why The Work is about the end of suffering.)

If a car runs over your leg and you're lying in the street with story after story running through your mind, chances are that if you're new to The Work, you're not going to think, *"I'm in pain"—is it true? Can I absolutely know that it's true?* You're going to scream, "Get the morphine!" Then, later, when you're in a comfort zone, you can sit down with a pen and paper and do The Work. Give yourself the physical medicine and then the other kind of medicine. Eventually, you can lose your leg and you won't see a problem. If you think there's a problem, your Work isn't done.

As long as we believe that we're our bodies, we don't have to know that we are infinite, our cells without limit, like music itself, free.

Are you afraid of being incontinent when you're old? Suppose your bowels let go in public—that would be normal for you. There would be no problem unless you believed that there was. When a baby does that, we think it's cute, it's healthy. Who would you be without your story? If it's not okay for your bowels to release anytime, anywhere, your Work isn't done. If that's what you need, it's the gift that reality will give you. Everything is for your homecoming.

Some people believe that if you're physically sick, you aren't spiritual enough, you aren't enlightened enough. If you were enlightened enough, they believe, you wouldn't have a stomachache or heart disease or cancer. I don't know about enlightenment, but even when I'm ecstatic, my stomach does what it does. And that seems to be how I live. My stomach is not my business; my thinking is my business, and not even that. Even if you have perfect peace, your body does what it does. "Sickness isn't spiritual"—can you absolutely know that that's true?

A doctor once took a sample of my blood and came back to me with a long face. He said he was bringing bad news; he was very sorry, but I had cancer. Bad news? I couldn't help laughing. When I looked at him, I saw that he was quite taken aback. Not everyone understands this kind of laughter. Later, it turned out that I didn't have cancer, and that was good news, too.

The truth is that until we love cancer, we can't love God. It doesn't matter what symbols we use—poverty, loneliness, loss—it's the concepts of good and bad that we attach to them that make us suffer. I was sitting once with a friend who had a huge tumor, and the doctors had given her just a few weeks to live. As

I was leaving her bedside, she said, "I love you," and I said, "No, you don't. You can't love me until you love your tumor. Every concept that you put onto that tumor, you'll eventually put onto me. The first time I don't give you what you want or threaten what you believe, you'll put that concept onto me." This might sound harsh, but my friend had asked me to always tell her the truth. The tears in her eyes were tears of gratitude, she said.

On one occasion in 1986 while I was getting a massage, I began to experience a sudden paralysis. It was as if all the ligaments, tendons, and muscles had tightened to an extreme. It was like rigor mortis; I couldn't make even the slightest movement. Throughout the experience, I was perfectly calm and joyful, because I didn't have a story that the body should look a certain way or move fluidly. Thoughts passed through, like "Oh my God, I can't move. Something terrible is happening." But the inquiry that was alive within me wouldn't allow any attachment to these thoughts. If that process were slowed down and given words, it would sound like this: "'You're never going to be able to walk again' — sweetheart, can you really know that that's true?" They're so fast, these four questions.

Eventually, they meet a thought at the instant of its arising.

At some point, after about an hour, my body began to relax and go back to what people would call its normal state. My body can never be a problem if my thinking is healthy.

How do you live when you believe the thought that your body should be different? How does that feel? "I'll be happy later, when my body is healed." "I should be thinner, healthier, prettier, younger." This is a very old religion. If I think my body should be different from what it is now, I'm out of my business. I'm out of my mind!

Your medicine is whatever appears now.

How do you know that you need cancer? You've got it. But to accept cancer doesn't mean that you lean back and do nothing. That's denial. You consult the best doctors you can afford, and you get the best treatment available. Do you think your body is going to heal most efficiently when you're tense and fearful and fighting cancer as an enemy? Or when you're loving what is and realizing all the ways in which your life is actually better because you have cancer, and from that calm center doing everything you can to heal? There's nothing more life-giving than inner peace.

We don't care if we have cancer. We don't care if we live or die. We just want this mind to stop. And in my experience it's not going to stop—but we can meet it with some understanding, and we can have freedom.

Nineteen years ago a doctor removed a large tumor from my face. I had found inquiry—inquiry had found me—so I didn't have a problem with the tumor. On the contrary: I was happy to see it come, and I was happy to see it go. It was actually quite a sight, and before it was removed I loved being out there in public. People would look at it and pretend not to be looking, and that tickled me. Maybe a little girl would stare at it, and then her parents would whisper to her and yank her away. Did they think they would hurt my feelings or that I was some sort of freak? I didn't feel like one. That tumor on my face was normal for me; it was reality. Sometimes I would catch someone looking at it, then he would look away, then after a while he would look again, then look away, look again, look away. And finally our eyes would meet, and we would both laugh. Because I saw the tumor without a story, eventually he could see it that way, too, and it was just funny.

I have a friend who didn't want to take medication. And I said, "God is everything, but not medicine?" God is medicine, too. So today she sees that it's a privilege to take medicine. She knows that whether it's working or not is not her business. The medicine says, "Take once a day." That's all she has to know. It's written on the bottle.

"I'm supposed to sleep at three o'clock in the morning"—is that true? I don't think so: I'm wide awake. When I wake up in the middle of the night, I get very excited. What could be better than sleep? Waking! I love lying in bed in the middle of the night with my eyes wide open, because that's what I'm doing. There's no thought that I should be doing anything else. I love all my thoughts.

No one can be too fat or too thin. That's not possible. It's a myth. It keeps you from the awareness of what is. It's the death of awareness. We don't want to believe thoughts like this, but we just don't know another way. So we do The Work, and even in a 500-pound body, we get lighter.

If someone says to you, "You're fat," they're right. Can you find it? And that's a candle over there; what's it going to do—die of shame? Don't call me a woman, or I'll go to war. Don't say I'm tall, or short. Do you understand? If someone says, "You should lose weight," I understand that. I've had the same thought myself. I find where they're right, I join them, and I give myself peace.

If I lose my right arm, how do I know I don't need two arms? I have only one. There's no mistake in the universe. To think in any other way is fearful and hopeless. The story "I need two arms" is where the suffering begins, because it argues with reality. Without the story, I have everything I need. I'm complete with no right arm. My handwriting may be shaky at first, but it's perfect just the way it is. It will do the job in the way I need to do it, not in the way I thought I needed to do it. Obviously, in this world there needs to be a teacher of how to be happy with one arm and shaky handwriting. Until I'm willing to lose my left arm, too, my Work's not done.

I'm not asking you to let go of your body, as if such a thing were possible. I'm asking you to own your body, to care for it, to take a look at your beliefs about it, to put them on paper, inquire, and turn them around.

When the mind thinks of death, it looks at nothing and calls it something, to keep from experiencing what it—the mind—really is. Until you know that death is equal to life, you'll always try to control what happens, and it's always going to hurt. There's no sadness without a story that opposes reality.

When the mind leaves a body, we throw it in the ground and walk away.

What is death? How can you die? Who says that you were ever born? There is only the life of an unquestioned thought. There is only mind, if anything. Live in the four questions for a while. That is where the world ends, until what's left comes back to explore the next concept. Do you continue after death? If you question your mind, you see that what you really are is beyond life and death.

No one knows what's good and what's bad. No one knows what death is. Maybe it's not a something; maybe it's not even a nothing. It's the pure unknown, and I love that. We imagine that death is a state of being or a state of nothingness, and we frighten ourselves with our own concepts. I'm a lover of what is: I love sickness and health, coming and going, life and death. I see life and death as equal. Reality is good; so death must be good, whatever it is, if it's anything at all.

The worst thing that can happen on your deathbed is a belief. Nothing worse than that has ever happened, ever.

The fear of death is the last smokescreen for the fear of love. We think that we're afraid of the death of our body, although what we're really afraid of is the death of our identity. But through inquiry, as we understand that death is just a concept and that our identity is a concept too, we come to realize who we are. This is the end of fear.

Loss is just a concept. I was in the delivery room when my grandson Race was born. I loved him at first sight. Then I realized that he wasn't breathing.

The doctor had a troubled look on his face and immediately started to do something with the baby. The nurses realized that the procedures weren't working, and you could see the panic begin to take over the room. Nothing they did was working—the baby wouldn't breathe.

At a certain moment, Roxann looked into my eyes, and I smiled. She later told me, "You know that smile you often have on your face? When I saw you look at me like that, a wave of peace came over me. And even though the baby wasn't breathing, it was okay with me." Soon afterward, breath entered my grandson, and I heard him cry.

I love that my grandson didn't have to breathe for me to love him. Whose business was his breathing? Not mine. I wasn't going to miss one moment of him, whether he was breathing or not. I knew that even without a single breath, he had lived a full life. I love reality, not the way a fantasy would dictate, but just the way it is, right now.

The great thing about death is that you do it on your own. Finally, you get to do something completely on your own!

There's no decision in death. People who know that there's no hope are free. The decision is out of their hands. It has always been that way, but some people have to die bodily to find out. No wonder they smile on their deathbeds. Dying is everything they were looking for in life. Their delusion of being in charge is over. When there's no choice, there's no fear. And in that, there is peace. They realize that they're home and that they've never left.

The parents and relatives of children who have died are especially attached to their stories, for reasons that we all understand. Leaving our sadness behind, or even inquiring into it, may seem like a betrayal of our child. Many of us aren't ready to see things another way yet, and that's as it should be. It takes a great deal of courage to see through the story of a death.

Who thinks that death is sad? Who thinks that a child shouldn't die? Who thinks that they know what death is? Who tries to teach God, in story after story, thought after thought? Is it you? I say, let's investigate, if you're up for it, and see if it's possible to end the war with reality.

I've sat with many people on their deathbeds, and after we do The Work, they always tell me that they're fine. I remember one very frightened woman who was dying of cancer. She had requested that I sit with her, so I came. I sat down beside her and said, "I don't see a problem." She said, "No? Well, I'll show you a problem!" and she pulled off the sheet. One of her legs was so swollen that it was at least twice the size of the other. I looked and I looked, and I still couldn't find a problem. She said, "You must be blind! Look at this leg. Now look at the other one." And I said, "Oh, now I see the problem. You're suffering from the belief that that leg should look like this one. Who would you be without that thought?" And she got it. She began to laugh, and the fear just poured out through her laughter. She said that this was the happiest she'd ever been in her entire life.

If we see the death of a child and feel turmoil inside, it's the story we're telling that causes us pain. This is obvious. If a child dies and no one tells us, we don't feel a thing. Somewhere a mother is crying at the loss of her child, and since we don't know that, we sit here having a wonderful time. How heartless of us!

I once went to visit a woman who was dying in a hospice. When I walked in, she was napping, so I just sat by her bed until she opened her eyes. I took her hand, and we talked for a few minutes, and she said, "I'm so frightened. I don't know how to die."

And I said, "Sweetheart, is that true?"

She said, "Yes. I just don't know what to do."

I said, "When I walked in, you were taking a nap. Do you know how to take a nap?"

She said, "Of course."

And I said, "You close your eyes every night, and you go to sleep. People look forward to sleeping. That's all death is. That's as bad as it gets, except for your belief system that says there's something else."

She told me she believed in the after-death thing and said, "I won't know what to do when I get there."

I said, "Can you really know that there's something to do?"

She said, "I guess not."

I said, "There's nothing you have to know, and it's always all right. Everything you need is already there for you; you don't have to give it a thought. All you have to do is take a nap when you need to, and when you wake up, you'll know what to do." I was describing life to her, of course, not death. Then we went into the second question of The Work: "Can you absolutely know that it's true that you don't know how to die?" She began to laugh and said that she preferred being with me to being with her story. What fun, having nowhere to go but where we really are now.

The questioned mind, because it's no longer seeking, is free to travel limitlessly. Thus it can never die. It understands that since it was never born, it has nothing to lose by allowing the unborn. It's infinite, because it has no desires for itself. It withholds nothing. It's unconditional, unceasing, fearless, tireless, without reservations. It has to give. That's its nature.

I have a friend who, after doing inquiry sincerely for a number of years, came to understand that the world is a reflection of mind. She was married to a man who was the love of her life, and one day, while they were sitting on their couch, he had a heart attack and died in her arms. After the first shock and the tears, she began looking for grief, and there was none. For weeks she kept looking for grief, because her friends told her that grief was a necessary part of the healing process. And all she felt was a completeness: that there was nothing of him that she'd had while he was physically with her that she didn't have now.

She told me that every time a sad thought about him appeared, she would immediately ask, "Is it true?" and see the turnaround, which washed away the sadness and replaced it with what was truer. "He was my best friend; I have no one to talk to now" became "I am my best friend; I have me to talk to now." "I'll miss his wisdom" became "I don't miss his wisdom"; there was no way she could miss it, because she *was* that wisdom. Everything she thought she'd had in him she could find in herself; there was no difference. And because he turned out to be her, he couldn't die. Without the story of life and death, she said, there was just love. He was always with her.

Until we know that death is as good as life, and that it always comes in its own sweet way, we're going to take on the role of God without the awareness of it, and it's always going to hurt. Whenever you mentally oppose what is, you're going to experience sadness and apparent separation. There's no sadness without a story. What is is. You *are* it.

Reality—the way that it is, exactly as it is, in every moment—is always kind. It's our *story* about reality that blurs our vision, obscures what's true, and leads us to believe that there is injustice in the world. I sometimes say that you move totally away from reality when you believe that there is a legitimate reason to suffer. When you believe that any suffering is legitimate, you become the champion of suffering, the perpetuator of it in yourself. It's insane to believe that suffering is caused by anything outside the mind. A clear mind doesn't suffer. That's not possible. Even if you're in great physical pain, even if your beloved child dies, even if you and your family are herded off to Auschwitz, you can't suffer unless you believe an untrue thought. I'm a lover of reality. I love what is, whatever it looks like. And however it comes to me, my arms are open.

I like to tell a story about a friend of mine who was waiting for a revelation just before he died, saving his energy, trying to be completely conscious. Finally his eyes widened, he gasped, and he said, "Katie, we are larvae." Profound awareness on his deathbed. I said, "Sweetheart, is that true?" And the laughter simply poured out of him. The revelation was that there *was* no revelation. Things are fine just as they are; only a concept can take that away from us. A few days later he died, with a smile on his face.

A lover of what is looks forward to everything: life, death, disease, loss, earthquakes, bombs, anything the mind might be tempted to call "bad." Life will bring us everything we need, to show us what we haven't undone yet. Nothing outside ourselves can make us suffer. Except for our unquestioned thoughts, every place is paradise.

My ninety-year-old mother is dying of pancreatic cancer. I'm taking care of her, cooking and cleaning for her, sleeping beside her, living in her apartment twenty-three hours a day (my husband takes me out for a walk every morning). It has been a month now. It's as if her breath is the pulse of my life. I bathe her, I wash her in the most personal places, I medicate her, and I feel such a sense of gratitude. That's me over there, dying of cancer, spending my last few days sleeping and watching TV and talking, medicated with the most marvelous painkilling drugs. I am amazed at the beauty and intricacies of her body, my body.

On the last day of her life, as I sit by her bedside, a shift takes place in her breathing, and I know: it's only a matter of minutes now. And then another shift takes place, and I know. Our eyes lock, and a few moments later she's gone. I look more deeply into the eyes that the mind has vacated, the mindless eyes, the eyes of the no-mind. I wait for a change to take place. I wait for the eyes to show me death, and nothing changes. She's as present as she ever was. I love my story about her. How else could she ever exist?

It's our beliefs about death that scare us to death.

A few months ago I was visiting Needles, the small desert town in southern California where my daughter, Roxann, lives. I was at the grocery store with her when some old friends of the family whom I hadn't seen for decades spotted me. "Katie!" they called out, and they came up to me, beaming. They hugged me, they asked how I was, I told them, and then they asked, "And how is your dear mother doing?"

I said, "She's wonderful. She's dead." Silence. Suddenly the smiles were gone. I saw that they were having a problem, but I didn't know what it was.

When Roxann and I were outside the store, she turned to me and said, "Mom, when you talk to people like that, they can't handle it." That hadn't occurred to me. I was just telling the truth.

Until you experience death as a gift, your Work's not done. So if you're afraid of it, that shows you what to question next. There's nothing else to do; you're either believing these childish stories or you're questioning them—there's no other choice. What's not okay about dying? You close your eyes every night and you go to sleep. People look forward to it; some people actually prefer that part. And that's as bad as it gets, except for your belief that says there's something else. Before a thought, there's no one, nothing—only peace that doesn't even recognize itself as peace.

When you're clear about death, you can be totally present with someone who's dying, and no matter what kind of pain she appears to be experiencing, it doesn't affect your happiness. You're free to just love her, to hold her and care for her, because it's your nature to do that. To come to that person in fear is to teach fear: she looks into your eyes and gets the message that she's in deep trouble. But if you come in peace, fearlessly, she looks into your eyes and sees that whatever is happening is good.

Dying is just like living. It has its own way, and you can't control it. People think, *I want to be conscious when I die.* That's hopeless. Even wanting to be conscious ten minutes from now is hopeless. You can only be conscious now. Everything you want is here in this moment.

We could say that I've already died. What I know about it is that when there's no escape, when you know that no one is coming to save you, beliefs stop. You just don't bother. So if you're lying on your deathbed and the doctor says it's all over for you and you believe him, all the confusion stops. There's no longer anything to lose. And in that sweet peace, there is only you. You are it, and that is presence.

Reality is the always-stable, never-disappointing base of experience. When I look at what really is, I can't find a me. As I have no identity, there's no one to resist death. Death is everything that has ever been dreamed, including the dream of myself, so at every moment I die of what has been and am continually born as awareness in the moment, and I die of that, and am born of it again. The thought of death excites me. Everyone loves a good novel and looks forward to how it will end. It's not personal. After the death of the body, what identification will mind take on? The dream is over, I was absolute perfection, I could not have had a better life. And whatever I am is born in this moment as everything good that has ever lived.

Nothing was ever born but a dream. Nothing ever dies but a dream.

III
ON PARENTS
AND CHILDREN

Here's what I've told my children: "You have the perfect mother. I'm responsible for all your problems, and you're responsible for the solutions."

Our parents, our children, our spouses, and our friends will continue to press every button we have, until we realize what it is that we don't want to know about ourselves yet. They will point us to our freedom every time.

"Mothers are supposed to love their daughters"—is that true? It's an old, old myth. It's as old as the dinosaurs. The way you can know it isn't true is that every time you believe it, you hurt. That's because it isn't your nature. When you believe it, you're in a lie.

You know how a mother bird pushes her chicks out of the nest? "You're out of here," she says. That's love. She doesn't say, "I love you: stay." She says, "I love you: fly." We can give you at least what a bird will give!

So how do you react every time you believe the lie that your mother should love you? Separation. Who would you be in your mother's presence if you didn't have the ability to think the thought that she should love you? At peace, a listener, just loving her the way she is. "Your mother should love you"—turn it around. *You* should love you. It's *your* job to love you. "I don't love myself, so you do it"—what's wrong with this picture? So *you* do it, and the way you do it is to stay present. Every time you do that, you fall in love with yourself, because you are the truth. Then, when your mother says something, all you hear is the sound of God, because God is everything, there isn't anything else. Until you can see your mother as God, your Work isn't done.

Parents can't be the problem. The Work is about being 100 percent responsible. This is very good news. It means there are no parents to change. There is only investigation.

You can't make people happy.

My daughter wanted a car. It was not an easy time in her life. She was just turning sixteen. She was so beautiful and dear and yet filled with self-hatred, guilt, and shame. I felt this was the perfect opportunity to make her happy, so I bought her a car. None of her friends owned cars; this would be really special. I thought the car was fabulous. I pictured her in it, and felt an all-consuming pleasure.

When I gave it to her, my heart was pounding with excitement. It was the gift of a lifetime, I thought, and I was giving her the key to happiness. But immediately I could see that something was wrong. She wasn't happy. It wasn't the car she wanted. (It was the kind of car that her friends would tease her about, she later said, and I'd had no way of knowing that.)

At the time, I was deluded enough to believe that she should be grateful, that she should love it, and that she was being difficult on purpose. I came to see that she was just like me. If anyone is going to make me happy, it has to be me, and she will find her own happiness or not. I came to see that it was all about me.

We're all five-year-olds. We don't know how to do this thing called life. We're just learning how.

If you think you're supposed to love your children, you're in big trouble. It just sets you up for shame and guilt. You're not supposed to love your children until you do. How do you react when you believe the thought that you're supposed to love them? Fear, depression, resentment, self-hatred. Maybe you feel like a freak, like there's something terribly wrong with you, some essential ingredient missing. Who would you be without the belief that you're supposed to love your children right now? You'd be free to love them or not, and to be a very good parent, whatever you're feeling right now. Then you could find your love, you could hear them now, you could be with them now, and you wouldn't have to do anything or be anything. Inquiry frees us from trying to be anything we're not.

"My children should be happy so that I can be happy?" That doesn't sound like love to me. I think I'll just skip them and be happy from here. It's a lot saner. It's called unconditional love.

God is another name for reality, and I am a lover of what is. If I lose my grandchild or my daughter, I lose what wasn't mine in the first place. It's a good thing. Either that or God is a sadist, and that's not my experience. I don't order God around. I don't presume to know whether life or death is better for me or for anyone I love. How can I know that? All I know is that God is everything and God is good. That's my story, and I'm sticking to it.

What's true for me is that in no way do I want my children's approval. That would assume I don't have it anyway. To want their approval would be to rape their minds. It would be to direct their minds to me when their minds are directed to where they're supposed to be.

"Parents are not supposed to attach to children"—what's the reality of it? Do they? So is it true that parents aren't supposed to attach? It's not true. I call it a flat-out lie. I call it that so it can be heard. How do you treat your mother or father when you believe that they're not supposed to attach to you? You pull away and feel superior. Who would you be without this story? Close your eyes. Look at your mother attaching to you. Look at her face, look at her body. Look at her without your story. What do you see? A beautiful human being, someone you love with all your heart. And nothing has happened except that you're seeing what is. When you attach to a story, you lose the awareness of that love.

Do children understand The Work? Absolutely. There are only concepts. There are no adults, there are no children. Concepts are ageless. Here's what children say: "My father should understand me." "My friends should listen to me." "Mommy shouldn't fight with Daddy." "I want you to love me." By the time they're four or five, children believe exactly the same stressful thoughts that adults believe. There are no new concepts. Children are just as confused as adults.

My children tell me what they want all the time. And I just hear them. What does that have to do with me? They're just expressing their wants. Those wants are their property. I have mine, and they have theirs. When they give me their wants, can I just listen, without thinking it's about me? That's what we all want from our parents: just someone to hear us and understand. We may think we want other things, but that's what we really want.

My job is to stay out of my children's business and to love them instead.

If your husband doesn't take care of the kids, does that mean that you don't get to do your own thing? Really? What stops you? How can anyone stop you from doing your own thing? If you want to do something without the kids, you can leave them. You can just leave them and go off and do what you want to do. But you don't. You stay with them because you want something more than to leave. Your husband has nothing to do with it. You can leave anytime. Isn't that fine to know? When you believe that you can't do what you want because of him, you're lost in a dream. It's the dream "I'm stuck" that makes you stuck. No mother ever has to stay with her children. We just like to tell the story of how we have to, and in that story we end up beating them, hating our husbands, getting divorced, going nuts. Who would you be without this lie?

Babies aren't born into the world of illusion until they attach words to things. When you're clear, it's great fun to observe that. I love being with my grandbabies, I love hearing what I teach them: "That's a tree." "That's a sky." "I love you." "You're Grandma's precious angel." "You're the most beautiful baby in the world." All these lies, and I'm having a wonderful

96

time telling them. If I'm creating problems for my grandchildren, they can question their stressful thoughts when they grow up. I am joy. I'm not going to censor any of it.

Your husband shouldn't go check his e-mail and be gone for hours? Hopeless! Children and family can't compete with e-mail! That's it. How do you treat him when you attach to this story that he should prefer you and the family to the Internet! Are you the teacher of shame and guilt? How does that feel inside you? Who would you be without the story that he should prefer you to the Internet?

People often ask me if I had a religion before 1986, and I say yes—it was "My children should pick up their socks." This was my religion, and I was totally devoted to it, even though it never worked. Then one day, after The Work was alive in me, I realized that it simply wasn't true. The reality was that day after day, they left their socks on the floor, after all my years of preaching and nagging and punishing them. I saw that *I* was the one who should pick up the socks if I wanted them picked up. My children were perfectly happy with their socks on the floor. Who had the problem? It was me. It was my *thoughts* about the socks on the floor that had made my life difficult, not the socks themselves.

And who had the solution? Again, me. I realized that I could be right or I could be free. It took just a few moments for me to pick up the socks, without any thought of my children. And an amazing thing began to happen. I realized that I loved picking up their socks. It was for me, not for them. It stopped being a chore in that moment, and it became a pleasure to pick them up and see the uncluttered floor. Eventually, they noticed my pleasure and began to pick up their socks on their own, without my having to say anything.

Like-minded? My whole family is like-minded. They lie on the floor, they walk, they sit, they tell stories. That's about it. None of the stories is true. They just have a wonderful time. It's a great movie. They tell the story of how I love them or I don't. It's all just a story.

Here's how a child listens: you tell him something, and he puts his own interpretation on what you said. That's what he hears. No one has ever heard you.

If one of my children were to say, "I hate you," I would say, "Let me be with that a minute. I understand—look how I treated you all those years. I understand that. What can I do? What do you suggest?" If he or she said, "Screw you with your spiritual talk! I never want to see you again," I wouldn't say lovingly, "I understand." I'm a listener. I go inside and understand. I don't have to share that understanding with them at that point. If I said, "I love you," it would be like taking a knife and sticking it into their heart.

You are the mother you've been waiting for. When you focus on your mother, you become motherless.

You enter this Work, and your children, your spouse, and your parents will give you everything you need to get free. The whole world will. It's all a reflection of you. It's perfect. There are no accidents.

You want your mother not to get the cancer back again. What for? So she can be a mother to you? Is she supposed to stay alive for your sake? She can't even live or die, except for you. Interesting, isn't it? Do you even care if she lives, except that that makes you happy? You think she likes living—what does that have to do with you? Nothing. Interesting, isn't it? You might go home and say, "Mom, I just discovered that I want you to stay alive so that I can be happy. And by the way, I love you."

I was a child at forty-three. I came to see that I didn't know anything. I didn't know how to live. I discovered this Work, and I noticed I was being lived. I was like a child, a toddler. It was so much fun! When we stay in The Work, we come to see we don't have to know anything. The whole world will give us everything we need.

Your child says you're stupid. He could be right! I can
go there. Who knows how to raise a child? All of us
are pretty stupid about that. All he said is that you're
stupid—why would you argue with that? Who would
be stupid enough to argue with someone they love,
if they had another way?

You could just say, "Sweetheart, what do you suggest? I do feel stupid. I love you, and I don't know
how to do it." That's the truth of it. We'd all act intel-
ligently if we knew how. And that's the power of this
Work—living the turnarounds, living the answers
that we find here. You could go home and say to your
son, "You've been telling me I'm stupid, and I found
it. I was the last to know. And what I'm stupid about
is that I don't know how to love you. I need your
help. I want to hear you."

Can I do what I wanted my parents to do? Can I give
myself what I wanted my parents to give me? This
is a life's work. Some of us don't know how. And we
expect our parents to have known how. Everything
you want them to give you, turn it around, and give it

101

to yourself. Life is good. I have myself now. And then everything I want, I give you, too. And I feel such joy. I come to see that that is the gift I give myself. But until I gave it to myself, I couldn't give it to you. And to give it to you is to give it to my very own self.

When my daughter, Roxann, attended her first workshop with me in 1993, there was a large group of therapists present. She was working on "the mother from hell"—which was how she had experienced me sometimes as she was growing up. She couldn't bear to look at me as she was doing her Work; it was hard for her even to hear the sound of my voice. I was the root of her problem, she thought, and I was also her salvation; she had to ask the monster for help, which made her furious.

At a certain moment she became very passionate and got right in my face and said I should have mothered her differently. I said, "That's not my job. Mother yourself, honey. *You* be the mother you always wanted."

Later she told me that that was the greatest gift I ever gave her. It turned out to be her freedom. I know the privilege of mothering myself. It's hopeless to see it as anyone else's job.

The bottom line is that your mother does love you—there's nothing she can do about that. Just don't expect her to be aware of it. Your mother loves you so much that she would withhold love so you can get this thing, this self-love thing. You can't love her until you do that. If I hate me, I hate my mother. If I love me, I love my mother. It's that simple.

Eventually, when a stressful concept appears, we're lit, we walk down the street like a thousand-watt lightbulb. A concept like "I need my mother to love me" comes in and we just laugh. We laugh because we're awake to that concept, and the next, and the next.

You can't disappoint another human being. And another human being can't disappoint you. You tell the story of how someone isn't giving you what you want, and you disappoint yourself. If you want something from your mother and she says no, that's it. You need to give it to yourself. This is good news, because it allows you to get what you want. If you don't have her to help you, you have *you* to help you. If she says no, it leaves you.

Self-inquiry is the mind giving itself its own story back. When we were children, the world said, "The sky is blue." So we said, "The sky is blue." We didn't stop to go inside and ask ourselves if it was true. We didn't know how. So we begin now. The mother says, "The sky is blue." And a wise child would go inside. *Can I really know that that's true?* No. I can see that it's my mother's religion; it just doesn't happen to be mine. And what she's got is equally as valuable as what I've got. So we love. She says it's blue, I say I understand. And I don't bother to tell her that it's not my experience. And if she asks me, I'm going to say, "You know, Mother, it's not my experience, and I love that you see that the sky is blue. We're compatible."

You know why we don't want our families to die? Because they hold the story of our past. Without them, we have to find a stranger, pretend to make friends with him, and tell him our story of the past so that when we're standing there with someone else to impress, we can turn and say, "Isn't that right?" To get him to hold up what is not true for us. When your family dies, there goes your history! It leaves you here, now.

I can be with my son and say, "Sweetheart, I see your pain. What can I do? I love you. If you can see a role for me to take here, to help you in any way, I'll do it. I love you. I'm here." And then I can hold him. But fear can't end fear. My pain can't end his pain.

And if he says, "Oh no, Mom, you can't help me. Go away," then I hear him. Good. How clear is that! So I go away. That leaves him to heal himself. He's with the master. I don't teach him that I'm the source of his happiness. That would be crazy. What would happen when I die? He'd lose the source of his happiness. To give him back himself—that's love.

It's painful to think that we know what's best for our children. It's hopeless.

"My mother should love me"—is that true? This is the death of a dream. Can you see one good reason to keep the story that *anyone* should love you, ever? Have you ever tried to love your perceived enemy? It's hopeless. Who would you be without this story that your mother should love you? You'd be you, without all that efforting. Without the mask, the façade. It feels like freedom to me.

Wanting your mother to love you is like being in a straitjacket. It's like being a dog on the floor just crawling and begging, with your tongue hanging out: "Love me! Love me! I'll be good! I'll be good!" Make a list of everything you want her to do for you, then do it for yourself, and do it now. This is the real thing. You want it from her? Turn it around and live it yourself.

If your wife dies, or if she leaves you and you have custody of your children, can you know that they won't be better off without their mother? This is a big one. "Children are much better off with their mothers"—is that true? This is the world's favorite religion, and can you absolutely know that it's true? I'm not saying that they aren't better off with her. This Work is an investigation, it's not about anything else, it's for

106

you to go inside and find out. I'm so greedy, I want it all, so I love, and I have it all. And any obstacle can only be a story. I investigate, and I am the experience of the awareness of love now—pure greed. When mothers don't remain with their children, how do I know that it's for their children's highest good? They aren't there! When mothers remain with their children, how do I know that *that's* for their children's highest good? There they are! Either that, or God is a sadist and the universe is chaos, and that is not my experience. That was my experience for forty-three years, but with this Work, I can only see perfect order. There is nothing terrible. Investigation is the way through to reality.

When you stay out of your family's business, they notice that you have your stuff together and that you're happy, so they start to follow. You've taught them everything they know, and now they begin to learn again. And that's what happened with my children; they just don't see a lot of problems anymore, because in the presence of someone who doesn't have a problem, they can't hold on to one.

Mothers are always right—they love that! Have you ever changed your mother's mind? It's not as though we have a choice. Your mother gets to be right all your life, but if your mind is open, *you* get to be free.

If your truth now is kind, it will run deep and fast within the family and will replace manipulation with a better way. As you continue to find your own way doing inquiry, sooner or later your family will come to see as you see yourself. There's no other choice. Your family is a projected image of your thinking. They're your story; nothing else is possible. Until you love your family without conditions, self-love is not a possibility, and therefore your Work isn't done.

How do you treat your children when you want them to love you and they don't? Can you see any reason that isn't stressful to want them to love you, or to want anyone on this planet to love you? If I have the thought that I want my children to love me, it isn't love. I want them to love whomever they love—I may as well, because that's what they do. I can't redirect it. I'm not a fool anymore. And people call that love, but I'm just a lover of what is. And I know the joy of loving, so I don't care how they direct it.

Who would you be without the story "I want them to love me"? To love your children is to love yourself. To love yourself is to love your children. The story "I want them to love me" just keeps you from the awareness of love.

When my children ask me what they should do, I say, "I don't know, honey." Or, "Here's what I did in a similar situation, and it worked for me. And you can always know that I'm here to listen and that I'm always going to love you, whatever decision you make. You'll know what to do. And also, sweetheart, you can't do it wrong. I promise you that." I finally learned to tell my children the truth.

Your family will see you as they see you, and that will leave you to do The Work on them all. How do you see *yourself?* That's the important question. How do you see *them?* If I think that they need The

Work, then *I* need The Work. Peace doesn't require two people; it requires only one. It has to be you. The problem begins and ends there.

"Children should love their parents"—is it true? That concept didn't work for me, so I gave it up. If it hurts, I give it up. I live internally. I always have. It's just that now I notice. My children should love me? Not ever. *I* should love my children: let me live the theory, especially when they don't call. If I want to hear my daughter, I call her, I hear her voice. I do it for my sake; she has nothing to do with it. I call, I get my daughter-fix, I am nourished, I hang up. I love when I do that.

Whose business are my children? Their business! When we're mentally out of our children's business, we have a shot at happiness, and so do they, because finally there's an example in the house.

How can you have rules and still stay out of your children's business? Drop the rules and find out! You'll find that your children, on their own, will live every rule you've ever taught them, and some of them you may not like. They are a perfect reflection of you. They turned out to be you.

Ultimately you don't have any control over your children. You don't have any control over anything. When you think you should and you see that you don't, the effect is depression.

Is it true that your children should be grateful that you were such a good parent? How do you treat them when they don't remember what a loving parent you've been? What do you say to them when they forget that you love them so unconditionally? How do you treat them when you want them to remember and be grateful and they want nothing to do with it? Offended? Hurt? Are you beginning to understand why they're not that crazy about you sometimes? This is our religion: "My children should be grateful." Turn it around: "*I* should be grateful that I was such a good parent." And be with that. It doesn't matter what the reason was; you were there when they were sick, you were there when they were well, you got them to school, you went to their performances, you read to them, you gave them birthday parties. It's not their job to be grateful, or even to remember. If you want a past, you keep it!

❧

Who would you be in the presence of your child if you didn't believe the thought that in the past you shouldn't have hit her? You think that guilt and shame are going to prevent you from hitting her again, but it's the opposite: you're using guilt and shame as weapons on yourself, you're causing internal violence to keep yourself from violence. It's internal violence to shame and blame yourself. If you don't believe the thought that you shouldn't have hit her, you aren't living in internal violence. We're not talking about right and wrong here. With the thoughts that you were acting out of at the time, weren't you doing the best you could? How do you know you should have hit her? You did. How did it feel? Not good. That's how you know you violated yourself. When you hit her, you are hitting yourself. She really is God in human form, here to teach you that.

112

If you want to alienate your friends and family, go around saying, "Is it true?" or "Turn it around" when they haven't asked you for help. You may need to do that for a while, in order to hear it for yourself. It's uncomfortable to believe that you know more than your friends and to represent yourself as their teacher. Their irritation will lead you deeper into inquiry, or deeper into your suffering.

When you stay present with your children, that's where abundance is. And when you stay out of their business, that's where everything you deserve in life is. When you're in presence, there's no story, and you are abundance; everything you ever wanted is here in this moment, and you come to trust it. And you come to trust that space so often that you just eventually hang out as that, because there is nothing that can move you out of it, not even a perceived child or a perceived anything.

Why would I give my children advice when I can't possibly know what's best for them? If what they do brings them happiness, that's what I want; if it brings them unhappiness, that's what I want, because they learn from that what I could never teach them. I celebrate the way of it, and they trust that, and I trust it.

If your daughter kills herself, whose business is that? When you think you know what's best for her, it's not love. How can you know what's best for her? How can you know that life would be better for her than death? You would deprive her of her whole path. Who do you think you are? There's no respect there.

If my daughter is going to take her life and I know about it, I'm going to speak to her and offer myself in whatever way she thinks would be useful. And if she has killed herself, I'm not going to think, *Sweetheart, you should have stayed here for my sake. I know you were suffering abominably, but you really should have stayed here and suffered so that I wouldn't feel terrible.* Is that love? Do you really want her to live in the torture chamber of her own mind? When our suffering gets too intense, we can inquire, and if we don't have inquiry, some of us just knock out our painful thoughts with a gun or pills or whatever it takes, but we have to shut this system down. And it's hell to open your eyes in the morning when you have this painful thought system going.

Unconditional love means that your children don't need your permission to live or die. How do you react when you believe the thought that she shouldn't have taken her own life? You get to experience hell. And who would you be if you didn't believe the concept that she shouldn't have taken her own life? Who would you be without the story? You can't have your daughter as long as you have a concept of her. When you get rid of the concept, you meet your daughter for the first time. That's the way this works.

The advice you've been giving your family and friends turns out to be advice for you to live, not us. You become the wise teacher as you become a student of yourself. It stops mattering if anyone else hears you, because *you're* listening. You are the wisdom you offer us, breathing and walking and effortlessly moving on, as you make your business deal, buy your groceries, or do the dishes.

Self-realization is the sweetest thing. It shows us how we're fully responsible for ourselves, and that is where we find our freedom. Rather than being other-realized, you can be self-realized. Instead of looking to us for your fulfillment, you can find it in yourself.

If your happiness depends on your children being happy, that makes them your hostages. So stay out of their business, stop using them for your happiness, and be your own happiness. And that way you are the teacher for your children: someone who knows how to live a happy life.

"My parents are responsible for my belief systems and my problems"—is it true? No, I'm the one who's responsible. Knowing this gives us what we always wanted: absolute control. And with this technology of going inside, it's the end of suffering, if we want to be free.

When my daughter, Roxann, was sixteen, she drank very heavily and also did drugs. This had begun to happen before I woke up with the questions in 1986, but I was so depressed then that I was totally unaware of it. After inquiry was alive in me, though, I began to notice her actions as well as my thoughts about them.

She used to drive off every night in her new red Camaro. If I asked where she was going, she would give me a furious look and slam the door on her way out. It was a look I understood well. I'd taught her to see me that way. I myself had worn that look on my face for many years. Through inquiry, I learned to become very quiet around her, around everyone. I learned how to be a listener.

I would often sit and wait up for her far past midnight, for the pure privilege of seeing her—just for that privilege. I knew she was drinking, and I knew I couldn't do a thing about it. The thoughts that would appear in my mind were thoughts like these: "She's probably drunk and driving, and she'll be killed in a crash, and I'll never see her again. I'm her mother, I bought her the car, I'm responsible. I should take her car from her" (but it wasn't mine to take; I'd given it to her; it was hers). "She'll kill someone, she'll crash into another car or drive into a lamppost and kill herself and her passengers." As the thoughts appeared, each one would be met with wordless, thoughtless inquiry. And inquiry instantly brought me back to reality. Here is what was true: woman sitting in chair waiting for her beloved daughter.

One evening after she'd been gone for a three-day weekend, Roxann came through the door with a look of great misery on her face and, it seemed to me, without any defenses. She saw me sitting there, and she just fell into my arms and said, "Mom, I can't do this anymore. Please help me. Whatever this thing is that you're giving to all these people who come to our house, I want it."

So we did The Work, and she joined Alcoholics Anonymous. That was the last time she did alcohol or drugs. The Work can complement any recovery program. Whenever she had a problem after that, she didn't need to drink or drug, and she didn't need me. She just wrote the problem down, asked four questions, and turned it around. When there's peace here, there's peace there. To have a way to see beyond the illusion of suffering is the greatest gift. I love that all my children have taken advantage of it.

Your family is an echo of your own past beliefs.

How do you react when you believe that someone you love is suffering? Whether she's suffering or not is *her* business, but how do you react when you believe the thought? You suffer, and then you have to leave the room; you have to leave the person you love. That thought keeps you out of the room you want to be in. So close your eyes, picture yourself in the room with your mother, without the belief that she's suffering, and without the belief that she's not supposed to. Is it fine to be in the room with her now? Of course it is.

I adore my children, and I adore my grand-children, and their suffering is their business. I let them have their suffering. They can live, they can die, and I love them, that's what I know. I love them enough to stay out of their business and be present. And I'm not being present on purpose; I just don't have a reason to leave the room when they're suffering, and in the presence of peace and love, it can't hold.

"My parents aren't supposed to judge me"—is that true? And aren't you making a judgment that your parents aren't supposed to judge? Well, they're just doing what you do. If you want them to stop, *you* try it. How do you treat your parents when they judge you and you're attached to the belief that they're not supposed to? That's our job: we judge. We've been told to stop judging for thousands of years, and it's still what we do. Haven't you noticed that it's hopeless? No matter how you isolate from them, move away, no matter what external or internal tantrum you throw, they still judge you. That's what they do. A dog barks, a cat meows, and parents judge.

Parents can only be wise when they stop teaching.

Your parents don't have to be alive for you to do The Work on them. No one has to be alive for you to do The Work on them. They live in your mind. That's where you heal yourself. Those of you whose family is gone, it's perfect. And those of you who still have your family living, it's perfect. No mistake.

Here's a very sweet way to communicate at home: just ask your child to read his or her Worksheet to you. There's no right or wrong here; this is communication. And after every statement, just say "Thank you." Nothing more. Love is a listener. This is about receiving. There's nothing more powerful than just to receive your daughter or son now. That is the giving; there's nothing more precious.

Did you take in every one of the statements? Did you find where it was true? How many times did you want to defend yourself? What does your child's opinion have to do with you? This is the end of war, inside your child, and therefore inside you.

Your parents are your projection—nothing more.

If you took your Worksheet to your mother or father and asked them just to be still all the way through and say "Thank you" after each statement, or if you just gave them each of the turnarounds to yourself, you would join them completely, because you can't say anything about yourself that they don't already know. On some level, they already know your greatest, darkest secret. It's no surprise.

It's not okay for me to yell at my son. I noticed that. It has nothing to do with the world's morality. So if I were ever angry at him, I would judge him, write it down, ask four questions, turn it around, and notice that he's not my problem—I am my problem. My children really love that I have this Work!

When your mind becomes clear, everything else follows. You step into the living of it, and then your job, your money, your children, and everything else follows. You get clear, and everything is cause and effect: I do this, I get that. That's the way of it.

Until I can understand myself, I can't even hear my parents. They are just my story. People who do this Work come to know their parents for the first time, even though their parents have been dead for thirty years.

Here's a meditation on a disapproving parent; you're welcome to do it if you think it would serve you:

Close your eyes. Now see your father, for example, with that disapproving look on his face. Now see yourself on your favorite chair. Now see him as a little boy. Now open your arms and invite him onto your lap. Did he come? Now hold him, smell his little head, and his hair. Just experience him there. Now tell him what you would like to tell him. Tell him you love him, if that's true. After you do this, you may have the most touching realizations. You may see that you care about your father the way you wanted him to care about you. It's the old turnaround trick: "I want him to love me" becomes "I want me to love him." We investigate the story, and the illusion is blown away. And it brings up the next story, so we can meet that one with understanding. And all the illusions start falling like dominoes.

I don't have relationships with my children anymore. I have intimacy instead.

If I have the thought *I want my mother to love me,* I'm insane. I turned it around: *I want me to love my mother.* Let me live what I thought should be so easy for her. "She should just drop her life and love me, I don't care what she wants—she should love me, I am clear, that's it." This isn't love. Can I just love without expecting anything in return? Can I live my own philosophy? And when I am in her presence, I am a very humble woman, because I really live it. But if I expect her to, I'm in big trouble. And if I'm not mentally dictating who she loves, it feels like self-love, because I see how I treat her when I want her love, and it's not a pretty sight. So I become the one who lives as love in our home.

And it seems to be contagious. I hated, and my children hated. I love now, and now my children love. It's effortless. That's why I say, with all assurance, "If you live it, we will follow." But you have to live it, because it's what you expect us to do. Don't expect your family to do anything that you can't do. When you learn it, then you can go teach it.

When you start to really live The Work, your family will follow. There's nothing you can do to stop them, because they're all living the way you have been teaching anyway, and they will continue to follow your teachings—not by what you say, but by the way you live. In the peace of that, they'll follow you. It may take a while, because they may not trust you or believe you, they may believe that you're in another tricky maneuver again. But if you live this Work, there's no trickery to it, it's the real thing, it's love. And eventually they come to trust that love. I can say anything to my children, and it's always my truth. And they know not to ask me if they don't want the truth. I am someone to trust.

If I see a mother hitting her child, for example, I don't stand by and let it happen, and I don't lecture the mother. She's innocently acting from a belief system she hasn't questioned. Because she believes her stressful thoughts—"The child is disrespectful," "He isn't listening," "He shouldn't talk back," "He shouldn't have done what he did," "He needs to be forced into submission"—she has to strike out. It's very painful to be confused. So when I see the mother, who is me, hitting the child, who is me, my way is to move to the mother, because she's the cause of the problem. I might go up to her and say, "Can I help?" or maybe "I know how painful it is to hit your own child. I've done that, too. I've been there. Would you like to talk about it?"

Love doesn't stand by—it moves with the speed of clarity. It includes both the mother and the child. To help the mother work with her thoughts is also to help the child. And I know that ultimately I'm not doing it for either of them, I'm doing it for myself, for my own sense of what's right. So activism becomes very personal, and in my experience it's more effective with a clear mind and no agenda.

When you investigate, eventually the dam breaks, and you're just left with open arms. One way to do this is to take your Worksheet and read the turnarounds to your father or mother. "Mom, I've been looking at you all my life, and today I began to look at me, and here is what I found: that I manipulate you, that I don't respect you, and that I'm learning how to, so please be patient with me, I'm really trying." There's nothing like presence; it's very exciting. And the way you treat your father or mother is the way you'll treat your husband and your children, because we're not dealing with people here; we're dealing with concepts. Living it, rather than talking it or thinking it, but living it, the living truth—it's a very good place to be.

One day a few years after I first found The Work inside me, my sons began to fight in our living room. I was sitting on the couch, very close to them. They were two grown men, in their twenties, and here they were on the floor, wrestling and pummeling each other and yelling, "Mom, Mom, make him stop!" All I saw were two men trying to connect, not knowing another way. I sat there just watching them, just loving them, and in that moment I didn't have the slightest thought of intervening. There was no doing, no trickery to it. And suddenly they noticed, and they stopped fighting. I loved that they found their own solution. That was the last time they ever fought.

Your children are there to give you your freedom; they are God disguised as your children, giving you everything you need. You have a great thing to work with. You have what I had to work with: my ex-husband, my mother, my children—and it was all me.

If my child has died, that's the way of it. Any argument with that brings on internal hell. "She died too soon." "I didn't get to see her grow up." "I could have done something to save her." "I was a bad mother." "God is unjust." But her death is reality. No argument in the world can make the slightest dent in what has already happened. Prayer can't change it, begging and pleading can't change it, punishing yourself can't change it, and your will has no power at all.

You do have the power, though, to question your thought, turn it around, and find three genuine reasons why the death of your child is equal to her not dying, or even better in the long run, both for her and for you. This takes a radically open mind, and nothing less than an open mind is creative enough to free you from the pain of arguing with what is. An open mind is the only way to peace. As long as you think that you know what should and shouldn't happen, you're trying to manipulate God. This is a recipe for unhappiness.

We love our children; there's nothing we can do about that, so we may as well succumb. And in that, they come to realize that they love us, there's nothing they can do about it, and they may as well succumb. I love that my grown children will still come into my arms, and that didn't happen until after 1986; it hadn't happened since they were young. Today it's the norm for them to come into my arms. We forget the age thing; we're just going for something else, the truth. It's nice to sit across from my children with no words, and be closer than close, closer than can be described.

We've never met our husbands, wives, mothers, fathers, children. Until we investigate our stories about them, we don't have a clue who they are. We're the last to know.

If you think we should be there for you, *you* be there for you! That's not our job. Our name is God; we don't move; we're never going to be there for you until you learn to inquire and turn it around. And that's not going to change. You can marry a saint and it's still not going to change: you won't even perceive that you're living with one.

If you think it was your parents who were out there, you're deluded. There was only God out there, disguised as your parents, giving you what you need. Every time you think your parents should be there for you, don't you experience pain? You miss the reality of it: they're not! Anytime you think you know what's best for you, it hurts. When you think they should be here when they're over there, you hurt, because the reality of it is that they should be where they are. You're trying to arrange the chessboard, and it has already been done! Checkmate!

There's only one way to handle God disguised as Mother: with unconditional love. Until you can see your mother as totally precious all the time, your Work isn't done. That's the beautiful thing about mothers: just in case you think you have it handled, we know what button to push.

I lost my children twenty years ago. I came to see that they were never mine to begin with. That was an extreme loss: they truly died to me. And my experience of them now is intimacy. What their experience of me is—that's none of my business. Do I want to be part of their experience? No, I'd rather have my own! How do I share my life? I don't. I invite them, and they say yes or no. They invite me, and I say yes or no.

Ultimately you lose everything. Everything that is thought to be external dies. Everything. You can't have anything. You can't have a husband—it's not a material husband. You can't have children—it's not material children. You can't have one concept. People think that nonattachment has to do with detaching from husband or children or house or car, but it's much more than that. It's a death.

My children pick up their socks now, they tell me. They understand now, they love me without condition, because when I became quiet they could hear themselves. Everything I undo, they have to undo; they are me, living out what I believed.

The apparent world is like an echo. The echo went out from me for forty-three years, and now it's coming back. It's all like a breath, like a lake when

131

you toss a pebble in, the ripples going out all those years and now they're coming back. I undid the turmoil, and my children are losing it, also. They're losing their attachment to so many of the concepts I taught them; they're becoming quiet. And that's what The Work does for everyone. That's what I mean by coming back into itself.

I'm someone to be trusted—without conditions. Even though my children may project it at times, there are no conditions. If they hate me, good. If they love me, good. I'm their story. Without their story, I don't exist.

We don't know how to change; we don't know how to forgive or how to be honest. We're waiting for an example. You're the one. You are your only hope, because we're not changing until you do. Our job is to keep coming at you, as hard as we can, with everything that angers, upsets, or repulses you, until you understand. We love you that much, whether we're aware of it or not. This whole world is about you. So, to put The Work into action, begin with the voice inside you that's telling you what we should do. Realize that it's actually telling *you* what to do. When it says, "He should pick up the socks," listen to the turnaround: "I should pick up the socks," and just do it. Stay in the flow that's effortless and unending. Pick them up until you love it, because it's your truth. And know that the only important house to clean is your mind.

At some point, you may want to go to the deepest suffering inside you and clear it up. Do The Work until you see your part in that suffering. And then go to the people you've judged, and apologize; tell them what you've seen about yourself and how you're working on it now. It's all up to you. Speaking these truths is what sets you free.

On Work and Money

For some of us, life is controlled by our thoughts about work and money. But if our thinking is clear, how could work or money be the problem? Our thinking is all we need to change. It's all we *can* change. This is very good news.

This Work is about doing business with clarity and vision, without any fear.

What you want money for is to buy happiness. The Work will give you happiness whether or not you have money. And it becomes very clear that money isn't that important. So you become unattached to money, and then it can't help but find you. That's a law.

Some people believe that fear and stress are what motivate them to make money. But can you really know that that's true? Can you be absolutely certain that without fear or stress as a motivator, you wouldn't have made the same money, or even more? "I need stress to motivate me"—who would you be if you never believed that story again?

The job you do out there in the apparent world is secondary. It's only a place for you to judge, inquire, and know yourself. Your true job is to appreciate what is; your primary profession is to be clear.

A material thing is a symbol of your thinking. It's a metaphor. We don't have to give up our things. They come or go; we have no control over that. We may think we do, but in reality we don't. Whoever started teaching that we need to let go of things, to detach from them, was a little confused. We notice that if we lose everything we're much freer, so we think that it's better to live impoverished. And then we notice that we're not free anymore. Everything changes. But when we work with our thinking, then to have great wealth is the same as to have nothing. That's the only freedom.

We think that because Jesus and the Buddha wore robes and owned nothing, that's how freedom is supposed to look. But can you live a normal life and be free? Can you do it from here, right now? That's what I want for you. We have the same desire: your freedom. And I love that you're attached to material objects, whether you have them or not, so that you can come to realize that all suffering originates from the mind, not the world.

Money is not my business; my thinking is my business. I don't have any other business.

You think that your life would be much better with that green car because having that car means something. What is it? It could just mean that you have a green car. You drive down the street and somebody says, "Oh my God, what is she doing with a green car?" Somebody else says, "Wow! She's got a green car!" Somebody else says, "Hmpf! How come she gets to have a green car?" It means whatever you think it means.

We don't attach to things; we attach to our stories about them. I don't hold on to my car; I hold on to the story about my car. "It's beautiful," "It's old," "It's falling apart," "It's in great running condition," "I need it to go to work," "I would be in trouble if I didn't have it," "It's cool," "It makes me look good," "It lets people know that I'm doing well"—that's what we're attached to. Without the story, no car. I don't mean we would or wouldn't physically have a car. Instead, reality would be "Woman getting into car going to work" or "Woman losing her job with something better coming along, and getting onto bus to go to work."

For people who enter this inner world, the world of inquiry, jobs become secondary. Freedom is everything. Jobs come, jobs go, companies rise and fall, and you're not dependent on that. Freedom is what we all want, and it's what we already are. And once you have inquiry, you can be as ambitious as you want in your job, you can shoot for the moon, because you can no longer fail. You realize that the worst that can happen is a concept.

The heart can sing, can't it?! That's why you wanted money in the first place. Well, you can skip the money part and just sing. It doesn't mean you won't have money, too. Can you do it for richer or poorer, as the world sees it? Yes, and all you've done is begin to tap into yourself—that's all that has happened. You've just answered a few questions from deep inside you.

Who would you be if you never believed the story "I need money" again? You've believed that if you didn't think you needed money, you would never have it. But the truth is that having money never had anything to do with thinking you needed it or not. There's nothing to know here. You don't have to know anything. There's ultimately nothing you can do to make money or to stop making money.

The Work is about internal cause and effect. It's not about external things.

After I found The Work inside myself—after it found me—I began to notice that I always had the perfect amount of money for me right now, even when I had little or none. Happiness is a clear mind. A clear and sane mind knows how to live, how to work, what e-mails to send, what phone calls to make, and what to do to create what it wants without fear.

Do you want your money to be safe and secure? Hopeless! Read my lips: hopeless! Banks burn, countries are bombed, people lie, they break their promises, they bend contracts. It's hopeless, hopeless.

How do you live when you believe the thought that your money should be safe? Who would you be without the thought "I need my money to be safe"? You might be a lot easier to be with. You might even begin to notice the laws of generosity, the laws of letting money go out fearlessly and come back fearlessly.

You don't ever need more money than you have. When you understand this, you begin to realize that you already have all the security you wanted money to give you in the first place. It's a lot easier to make money from this position. The money comes because it's with the appropriate keeper.

The concept "I want my money to be safe" puts you in the position of the miser. So it goes out miserly, it comes back miserly. And even if it comes back in the billions, it still doesn't feel that way, because you've attached to the concept "I have to make it safe." So you're not the keeper of it, you're afflicted with it. *It* is keeping *you*.

When you live the turnaround "I want my *thinking* to be safe," you don't need money. You have all the security you wanted money to give you in the first place. Money is like air—it's everywhere. There's nothing you can do not to have it. And if you don't have it, it's because you don't need it. So you can skip the money part and be free! You don't ever need more money than you have.

The belief "I have to work" has never been true; it's the lie you hold on to so that you can keep yourself from the joy of the gift that you give. No one has to work. No one has ever had to.

"My money shouldn't go to other people without my permission"—is that true? That's a wonderful myth. And what's the reality of it? *Does* your money go to other people without your permission? Of course it does. So the statement is a lie. Because you're a miser with your money, sometimes you think you have control over where it goes. But all you're doing is proving to yourself that this lie works, the lie that you have control, so you try to get tighter control. It's a godless place. It leaves you alone, with no connection. And that's terrifying, and really lonely. In that space, when you have money, you attribute that to your miserliness. So you're teaching yourself that you have the money because you're a miser, and it's an illusion. You have it because you have it. You're not in control. A tree puts out leaves without your help. A baby is born and you didn't even know. This is abundance. You did nothing to get it.

Wealth and poverty are in your own mind. You could be rich with ten dollars or poor with a billion dollars. It's just your story about money that strikes terror in your heart. Has there ever been a time in your life when you didn't have enough? There's abundance all around you and you don't even notice. Not only do you have clothes, but you have clothes under them; not only do you have ears, but you have earrings. Who would you be without the thought that you don't have enough? Who would you be without this belief that you think will scare you into making money? Even though you don't believe in slavery, you are the slave and the slave owner. And it wears you out brutally, until you don't even want to go to work.

Go to the top of your Worksheet and read everything you wrote, substituting the word *mother* for *money*. Are you beginning to see how we only attach to beliefs, that there's no such thing as money or mother or any of it? The concept is our god. We investigate the concept, and we lose the whole world, which never existed in the first place. It's not the money or the mother that is the problem. It's the concept you're attached to.

You haven't been taking care of yourself; you've been taking care of your money. You think, *I'll take care of myself after I have enough money, after I get it secured. I'll be happy then.* And "then" never comes.

"Money is exciting and adventurous"—is that true? It just sits there! It's even boring—all those little faces. Money does nothing; it just sits there. It doesn't think, it doesn't feel, it doesn't know, it doesn't care, it doesn't play favorites, it just is. A piece of metal. A piece of paper. Even gold bullion is just that. The story you put onto it is what thrills you, what interests you, what scares you. You tell the story of what money is doing, what it's going to do, how it should come and go, and you heaven or hell yourself. But money just sits there.

Without a story, it's just not personal. You get to the place where you don't care whether you live or die, because you're having so much fun investigating these concepts. Someone tells you, "You don't have any money," and you say "Oh! I didn't know that." Or they ask, "How come you have millions of dollars?" and you say, "I do?" The internal world is so fine. There's nothing that can compete with it.

You are your own boss. Even if you have the most menial job in the world, you are your boss. And if you don't like your job, welcome to The Work.

Can you really know that your highest good is to be an artist? How do you react when you believe that thought? You refuse to be content in a job less lofty than that, and when you get a job, you hate it because you think you're just marking time until you can devote yourself to your art. So you're always living in the future, and you're never present. Who would you be without your story that you're supposed to have a career as an artist? You'd be that saint down there flipping burgers or scrubbing floors. You'd be in my favorite position: the position of servant.

Poverty is internal. Every time you think you know something, you're experiencing poverty.

"You're supposed to be seen at work, for who you are"—is that true? Did you put it in your job description? Does your contract say, "If you do this and this and this, then we'll see you"? Put that in the contract before you take the job. Tell the boss, "Yes, I understand the requirements here, and I have one of my own: I need to be seen at work." You go to work and you think we should see you. We're just doing our job here, people pay us, we've made a commitment, but according to you we should take time out to see our legal secretary, she needs to be seen. That's what you're asking; you're asking us to drop our integrity, so that you can be seen. When you think we should see you and we don't, you disconnect, and what does that have to do with us? How do you react when you believe this insane thought that you need to be seen? You go blank, you begin to hate your job and call it us.

Who would you be if you didn't believe the thought that we should stop what we're doing and see you? You might be someone who doesn't stop to see if we are seeing you. You might be someone

146

who stays in her own business. And you might be someone who loves her job. You would see your job instead of this theory that we should see you. And then when you got your paycheck, you would love it, because you'd know that you had earned it and you hadn't cheated.

No job has ever bothered you; only your thinking has. You only have one job: to come into alignment with your thinking. And the way you do that is that you write it down, then apply four questions and a turnaround, and go inside for your answers.

The future shows me why the money comes in. It's backward. I'm a conduit. There's nothing I can do not to have everything I need.

If you don't know what the truth is, it will be there for you. It's called reality. Reality—that's the last place we look. How does it feel when you have one job and you think you should be doing something else? It's very painful. Who would you be without the story "I should be doing something different"? Doing what you do, present, efficient, available. And when you are that clear as an employee, you don't last long in that position; they promote you. It's called integrity. It's a well that's bottomless, it's so vast. Turn it around: "I shouldn't be doing something different." Not now. Maybe it will change, but right now this job is good. The only thing that's not good about now is a story that would keep you from it.

Many of us are motivated by a desire for success. But what is success? What do we want to achieve? We do only three things in life: we stand, we sit, we lie horizontal. Once we've found success, we'll still be sitting somewhere until we stand, and we'll stand until we lie down or sit again.

Success is a concept, an illusion. Do you want the $3,900 chair instead of the $39 one? Well, sitting is sitting. And for the word *chair* you could substitute *car* or *house* or *business*. You can only sit in one place at one time. If I think that I should have a different chair, just to use that metaphor, I am insane! I'm wanting two things at once, and confusion is the only suffering. "I want another chair" is a lie. What I want is *this* chair, obviously, because it's the one I have. So I'm no longer confused. How do I know I want this chair? I'm sitting in it.

The truth is that you really love the job you think you hate. Except for your beliefs, it's the job for you. How do I know? It's the one you have! You could own the company you're working for if you just realized that you're not there because you have to be at that job. If you drop all your beliefs around it, we want you, we'll pay you anything, you're irresistible, you're love in action.

The thought "I have to go to work" makes your life a war zone. Whereas if you just wake up knowing to go to work, you just go, you go in peace, and work is a pleasure. But when you argue with reality, the beliefs pile up, and the office becomes a sweatshop.

When should you fire someone? That's simple: when you want the job done. Do you want the job done or not? Just stop fooling yourself. This way you can talk to that person from a position of understanding, because you're being responsible for your own life.

I once did The Work with an executive who said, "My assistant has been with me for ten years. I know she doesn't do the job well, but she has five children."

I said, "Good. Keep her here so she can teach the rest of your employees that if they have enough children, they can work for you, whether they do their job well or not."

And he said, "Well, I just can't fire her."

I said, "I understand that. So put someone qualified in her position, send her home to her five children who need her, and send her a paycheck every month. That's more honest than what you're doing now. Guilt is expensive."

When the executive read his Worksheet to the woman, she agreed with every single thing he had written about her job performance, because it was clear and true. And I said to her, "What do you suggest? What would you do if you were *your* employee?" People usually fire themselves when they realize what's going on, and that's just what she did. She found a similar job in another company, closer to her home, where she was able to be both a good assistant and a good mother. The executive realized that he had never investigated the thoughts that led him to be "loyal" to an assistant who, in reality, had been just as uncomfortable with the situation as he was.

Your job is not about making money or working with people or impressing your friends or getting respect. The job is about your freedom. Everything—every man, woman, and child, every tree, every stone—is about your freedom. It's all God giving you what you need so you can get honest one time.

If everyone knew to do the Work, there would be no unemployment. How could there be any unemployment since there is only one job: to know yourself?

Your fears are nothing more than a lack of integrity, that's all, there's no mystery. Write them down, inquire, and notice how they just don't arise anymore; and if they do, they have encountered a friend, and there's peace. Fear is lack of integrity, and the way you know this is that when you're in a lie, you experience discomfort. Life is simple, until you lose your internal integrity, and then it hurts. The feeling of discomfort will let you know. It says, "Sweetheart, take a look, get honest."

If you really believe in your product and in yourself, there's no selling, ever. When you think you know what's best for us, you hurt. The reality is that you don't know what's best for us. I don't think for a moment that I have something you need. If I believed that, I'd be insane. What I want for you is what you want for yourself. The only valuable skill is getting real.

If your mind is clear, you can walk out the door right now, with no friends, no job, no family, no money, no anything, and live absolutely happily. You can't *not* have abundance in paradise. In the stillness beyond belief, everything is known: where to go, what to do, when. All of it. The way I live is that I don't ever have to know anything again—not ever.

There is no way you can't have the best business on this planet. No one stops you but you—that's the only possibility. Your employees aren't responsible for your success; you are. And for those of you who are employees, it doesn't matter whom you work for: if you do this Work, there is no way you can't be a success.

When you've become a total success in business and have more money than you could ever spend, what are you going to have? Happiness? Isn't that why you wanted the money? Let's take a shortcut that can last a lifetime. Answer this question: Who would you be without the story "My future depends on making a lot of money"? Happier. More relaxed. With or without the money. You'd have everything you wanted money for in the first place.

You think that the belief that you need money keeps you safe. "If I dropped the belief, who would be there to scare me into making money?" Without the belief, you think, you wouldn't be motivated. But can you know that? Can you know that if you didn't try to scare yourself into making money, you wouldn't have any, you would just sit there like a nonproductive lump? And how do you react when you believe the thought that you would have no inspiration to make money? I've heard of incentives, but people take this a bit far.

It's good that you think you're going to lose your job. This is exciting. Do The Work, live The Work, notice, and know that if you lose your job, there is something better waiting for you. But when you're stuck in a belief, you're blind. There has to be something better, because there is only goodness in the universe. "My life would be much better if I don't lose my job"—can you absolutely know that that's true? There's nothing more exciting than living on the edge and being aware of it.

My son lost a really big record contract, and he called me and said, "Mom, I'm so excited. I lost a wonderful contract, and I'm so excited to see what's going to come that's better than that!"

I love it that the stock market isn't going to cooper-ate in giving you a million dollars, if that's what it takes to bring peace and true happiness into your life. That's what everything is for. It leaves you to your own solution. So when you get all this money and you're happy, totally happy, what are you going to do? You're going to sit, stand, or lie horizontal. That's about it. And you're going to witness the internal story you're telling now if you haven't taken care of it in the way that it deserves: to meet it with understanding, the way a loving mother would meet her child.

If I had a lot of money and someone told me you were my friend because of that, I would say, "Good." I don't care why—your motives are not my business, you're my friend. Only *my* motives are my business, and thank you for being my friend. It doesn't matter why you're my friend; the fact is that you're there for me, you care about me, and the reason isn't my business.

If you ask me for something and it's honest for me to give it, I will, and if it isn't honest for me, I won't. To think that you're motivated by my money is to separate from you. And if I'm not honest with my no's and yeses, it could be that I'm trying to buy your friendship with my money. But when I'm clear, you're my friend again, inside me. I don't care what brings us together. If I think I know your motives, I have just cost myself a friend.

You can sit there and think, *Oh, I need to do something with my stocks,* and then you can inquire. "Is it true? No, I can't really know that." So you just let the process have you. You just sit there with what your passion is, and read, and watch the Internet and let it educate you. And the decision will come from that, at the perfect time. It's a beautiful thing. You'll lose money because of that decision, or you'll make money. As it should be. But when you think you're supposed to do something with your stocks and imagine that you're the doer, that's pure delusion. Just follow your passion. Do what you love, inquire, and have a happy life while you're doing it.

The next time you give your children money, realize that the receiving is in the giving. There's nothing more to receive than that. If you touch it again, it's hot! The receiving is in the moment you give it. That's all you get. It's over. If you have one expectation, one desire for them to be grateful, you lose the gift. Love is an impulsive act. It's free. It's the story you tell about it afterward that's your poverty. My generosity is what's mine; the story you tell about it has no effect on me. What does that have to do with me? But my gift—that's what I receive. Attaching to these insane stories, without investigation, is how you cost yourself the gift that you are.

When you lose something, you've been spared—either that or God is a sadist. How do I know I don't need the money? It's gone! I've been spared: what I would have done with that money would obviously have been much less useful for me than losing it.

Can you find one valid reason to keep the story that your husband shouldn't make a mistake with his business? I can't find one that doesn't hurt. Who would you be without the story? He might come in and say, "Oh my God, I made a huge mistake, I lost all our money," and you could say, "I understand that; we all make mistakes. What do you suggest? I'm here for you." And that's what we ultimately do anyway.

On the other side of all the terror and blame, we say, "I love you. How can I help?" That's who we are. What The Work does is cut to the chase. Who would you be without the story that he shouldn't make a mistake? He'd have a home to come to, and you would be that home, and you would have a home to go to in him, which is a comfortable place.

Doing The Work on job-related issues can have far-reaching consequences. When I work with corporations, I sometimes invite all the employees to judge each other. This is what employees and bosses have always wanted: to know how they look from each other's point of view. And then, after the judgments, they all do The Work and turn it around. The result can be a startling increase in clarity, honesty, and responsibility; and this, in turn, inevitably leads to a happier, more productive, and more efficient workforce.

If I hire you and you don't meet the requirements, I thank you for all that you've offered, and I fire you. Maybe I talk with you first to see if there's something about your job performance that I may have missed. And if you don't meet my requirements, I thank you, because I know you've done the best you could, and I fire you, and I hire someone who's qualified to do what I want.

It's not up to my employees to accomplish what I want; it's up to me. I'm the boss. And the reason that firing you is so kind is that I've just released you from a torture chamber and allowed you to move into a space where you *are* qualified. And because of my clarity and kindness, the position is open for the right person to move into it. Anything less than that is masochism: it's unkind to you and to me.

The reason I love this Work is that we begin now. It's much more fun than running a business; you're running something much more important. And your company will follow, because when the boss is clear, the employees become clear. The more clarity you live within your company, the more you get. Your employees have to be attracted by that, even if they're not aware of it. There's nothing more efficient than a boss in whose presence people can be themselves.

Whenever you think that your needs are not being met, you're telling the story of a future.

Financial security is only a state of mind. The worst that can happen is a belief about what losing all your money would be like. Close your eyes, get your shopping cart, find your city, you're out there on the streets, check out your environment, make friends with what you see, go into your worst nightmare. You're a bag lady. There's no way out. No one is coming to save you. It's your projection about how life is on the streets that scares you. When you get there—and I've been there—the worst that can ever happen turns out to be the sweetest thing.

My first experience of freedom from this fantasy was when it was very cold outside; it had frozen and rained and snowed, and I was in a warm place having a cup of tea. And I saw a homeless man who had obviously slept outside all night. He just had a thin blanket around him, and I couldn't imagine how he hadn't frozen to death. But sanity doesn't suffer. When the mind is clear, there's no time when we can't go to some warm place and get out of the cold. In this stillness, we know where to go and what to do. But with a confused mind, we can't see that, and we chase after money and we save it and we're miserly with it, so that this nightmare doesn't happen, and the nightmare itself is an illusion. This homeless man didn't have enough sense to come out of the cold; his mind wasn't clear enough.

Here is how you stay cold: it's freezing outside, you have only a very light blanket, and you think, *I could go into this building but no, I look too shabby, they'll never let me in.* Can you see how inquiry won't hold that? "They'll never let me in"—can you really know that? How do you react when you believe that they won't let you in? You freeze. "There's no place to go"—is that true? Who would you be without the thought? Clear enough to step in out of the cold, to know where to go and when.

Your thinking is the worst that can happen, and you scare yourself so that you have to go out and make money and be a miser. "I don't want to do God's will and be a bag lady on the streets; I am of much more value over here in my nice warm home"—can you really know that?

You're the one calling the shots on what is a mistake in your business and what isn't. In reality, there are no mistakes, there are no accidents. (But that's a bit advanced for some of us.)

Does the wind blow? Did you experience rain today? That's it: What is is. We make mistakes, we don't; the wind blows, it doesn't; it is what is. Your story about it—that's where the heaven or the hell is. But one thing you can count on is that people will make what you consider mistakes. You can fire them, you can yell at them, you can divorce them, and the person in front of you is going to make a mistake, count on it. So all you can really do is to sit and investigate that concept. That's as good as it gets. If you believe that people shouldn't make mistakes, welcome to hell.

The story "I need more money" is what keeps you from realizing your wealth. Whenever you think that your needs are not being met, you're telling the story of a future. Right now, you're supposed to have exactly as much money as you have. This is not a theory; this is reality. How much money do you have? That's it—you're supposed to have exactly that amount. If you don't believe it, look at your checkbook. How do you know when you're supposed to have more? When you do. How do you know when you're supposed to have less? When you do. Realizing this is true abundance. It leaves you without a care in the world, as you look for a job, go to work, take a walk, or notice that the cupboard is bare.

There is no business where The Work doesn't apply. I hear from CEOs, barbers, therapists, prison workers, and doctors who are finding that whatever else their jobs are, they are ways of giving people back to themselves.

If I didn't have money, I would do whatever it took to pay my bills. I just wouldn't need a plan about how that was going to look. It would come to me to mop floors, to clean houses, and I'd love doing that. And one thing would lead to another, one job would lead to another, I would do it all for my own sake, and enjoy it all. I can't not be wealthy. It has nothing to do with money.

You can take any job, anytime, and except for your belief systems, money is not a problem. You can work in a hamburger joint and make minimum wage. And if you just hold on to your integrity, without any beliefs about how that should look, eventually you could own the whole chain. Because we're attracted to that kind of integrity, and money can't buy it, so we will give you anything to be in your presence.

If I get myself into trouble, I get myself out of it. And if I file for bankruptcy, I eventually pay off every debt I owe, because living in this way offers me the freedom I'm looking for. I don't care if I can only pay a dime a month. I act as an honorable person, not because I'm spiritual, but because it hurts if I don't.

Your job is to appreciate what is, and that includes appreciating your boss. To appreciate him is to appreciate yourself.

I never lend people money. I *give* them money, and they call it a loan. If they repay it, that's when I know it was a loan.

God's will for me is that I not own anything, however many possessions I apparently have. So I love it when people come and steal all my things; that way, I can see if there's one little attachment left in me, one little place of entitlement. Because there is only one joy in life: undoing myself.

You can't let go of your possessions; it doesn't work like that. You investigate your beliefs about father or mother, for example, and something happens that's totally unrelated, and you experience freedom. Thieves take everything you own and people are saying, "Oh, you poor thing, how terrible for you," and you don't feel terrible at all, you feel amused, you feel exhilarated, because you're awake to all the stressful thoughts that might arise. And you haven't done anything but let go of a belief.

I knew a woman who had megabucks. Her father adored her, she adored him, and one way that he showed his love was by giving her money. It was an incredible gift, but she took it from herself and lived in poverty because she believed she didn't deserve it. She believed that she had to do something to deserve all that money. And she found out that that thought was a way of being separate from her father and from herself.

There's a huge prejudice about people with money, and that's how we separate. She found out that she was just like her father; she was overindulgent; she kept on giving her money to husbands who didn't earn anything after they married her. Her father gave it to her, and she gave it to her husbands. It's called generosity; it's called love. And what she came to see was that she did it for her own sake, and to withhold it was where the pain was.

When I receive money, I am thrilled, just thrilled, because I'm fully aware that it's not mine, that I'm just a channel. I'm not even the caretaker. I get to be the observer of it. The moment I get it from over there, a need for it appears here. It's amazing.

How do you react when you believe the thought that if you had more money you'd be happier? You get to be unhappy now. You get to put your whole life on hold until you have more money. It's so much easier to be happy now. And that happiness is what The Work brings you in every moment, until eventually the space gets so wide that it becomes very clear how to make money, it becomes clear that you have it, that there is nowhere to go, no one going, and that you are where you always wanted to be. This is what all your thinking has brought you to. And if you are here fully, *here* contains everything you ever wanted. It's very sweet, because *here* is where you always are.

Being present means living without control and always having your needs met.

The whole world will tell you that you shouldn't be messy. This is our religion. But all the punishment in that concept, "I shouldn't be messy," hasn't worked yet. A messy mind is a messy life. It's hopeless to try to clean up your house, your office, your desk. But if you clean up your thinking, then cleaning up your office and your house is effortless. You work with the mind, and your life gets transformed. The mess in your office is not the problem. Your boss can say, "I'll give you a million dollars if you clean up your mess for one year," and that still won't work, because you don't know how. "I need to clean up my mess"? No, you need to clean up your thinking. There isn't anything else to clean up. And when you do, the rest will follow.

Abundance has nothing to do with money. Money is not your business; truth is your business. You're supposed to have more money than you have? I don't think so. You're supposed to have less money? I don't think so. You're supposed to have exactly what you have.

Money is a wonderful metaphor. It flows from here to there, through all countries, through phone systems and wires. It shows us how to be, mentally: how to flow, how not have any barriers, how to take all forms. It shows how easy it is to come and go, all the time. It's a great guru. If you did what money does, you'd be completely in love with what is.

In my experience, there's nothing more fun than self-realization. Isn't that why we want money—to bring us happiness and peace? And the beautiful thing about inquiry is that you can do it from wherever you are—while you're making money, while you're at home, while you're with your lover, while you're with yourself. Life is internal.

ON SELF-REALIZATION

Life on the other side of inquiry is so simple and obvious that it can't be imagined. Everything is seen to be at its best, just the way it is. Hope and faith aren't needed in this place. Earth turned out to be the heaven I was longing for. This is the unimaginable life that I live, that we all live.

As closely as I can describe it in words, I am your heart. I am what you look like inside yourself. I am the sweetest place that you come from. Whether you love me or hate me depends on whether you love or hate yourself. I am no one. I am just a mirror. I am the face in the mirror.

As you lose the filter that I call a story, you begin to hear your own self at a higher level, and it starts to sound like me, only in its own way: brilliant, itself. There's a resonance that doesn't ever leave the center. You come to honor it, because you come to realize that you have no authentic life outside it.

I have no ideas about whether you should or shouldn't suffer. I respect your path as much as I respect my own. I understand if you're mesmerized by your story and want to hold on to it. If you say that you *don't* want to suffer, I'm there for you. Through inquiry, I'll meet you as deeply as you want to go. Whatever you say, I'll meet it. Whatever you ask for, I'll give. I love you, because I'm totally selfish. Loving you is simply self-love.

My experience is that confusion is the only suffering. Confusion is when you argue with what is. When you're perfectly clear, what is is what you want. So when you want something that's different from what is, you can know that you're very confused.

I am here to take the mystery out of everything. It's simple, because there really isn't anything. There's only the story appearing now. And not even that.

The Work always brings us back to who we really are. Each belief investigated to the point of understanding allows the next belief to surface. You undo that one. Then you undo the next, and the next. And then you find that you're actually looking forward to the next belief. At some point, you may notice that you are meeting every thought, feeling, person, and situation as a friend. Until eventually you are looking for a problem. Until, finally, you notice that you haven't had one in years.

Through inquiry, we discover how attachment to a belief or story causes suffering. Before the story there is peace. Then a thought enters, we believe it, and the peace seems to disappear. We notice the feeling of stress in the moment, investigate the story behind it, and realize that it isn't true. The feeling lets us know that we're opposing what is by believing the thought. It tells us that we're at war with reality. When we notice that we're believing a lie and living as if it were true, we become present outside our story. Then the story falls away in the light of awareness, and only the awareness of what really is remains. Peace is who we are without a story, until the next stressful story appears. Eventually inquiry becomes alive in us as the natural, wordless response of awareness to the thoughts and stories that arise.

If you want reality to be different than it is, you might as well try to teach a cat to bark. You can try and try, and in the end the cat will look up at you and say, "Meow." Wanting reality to be different than it is is hopeless. You can spend the rest of your life trying to teach a cat to bark.

I am a lover of what is, not because I'm a spiritual person, but because it hurts when I argue with reality. No thinking in the world can change it. What is is. Everything I need is already here now. How do I know I don't need what I want? I don't have it. So everything I need is supplied.

You can't have an up without a down. You can't have a left without a right. This is duality. If you have a problem, you must already have the solution. The question is, Do you really want the solution, or do you want to perpetuate the problem? The solution is always there. The Work can help you find it. Write down the problem, question it, turn it around, and you have the solution.

I am your heart. I am the depth you don't listen to: in your face, from here. It had to get louder, because your beliefs block it out from there. I am you on the other side of The Work. I am the voice so covered up with beliefs that you can't hear it inside yourself. So I appear out here, in your face—which is really inside yourself.

Fear has only two causes: the thought of losing what you have or the thought of not getting what you want. In either case, the worst thing that can ever happen is a story. Nothing you need can be taken from you.

And no one can ever have anything you need. Need is a story you tell yourself. It's a lie that causes you pain and separates you from yourself. It's a wanting what is not that separates you from what is.

A feeling is like the mate to a thought appearing. They're like a left and a right. If you have a thought, there's a simultaneous feeling. And an uncomfortable feeling is like a compassionate alarm clock that says, "You're in the dream." It's time to investigate, that's all. But if we don't honor the alarm clock, then we try to alter and manipulate the feeling by reaching into an apparent external world. We're usually aware of the feeling first. That's why I say it's an alarm clock that lets you know you're in a thought that you may want to investigate. If it's not acceptable to you, if it's painful, you might want to do The Work.

When you're mentally out of your business, you experience immediate separation, loneliness, and fear. If you're lonely or sad, you may ask yourself, "Whose business am I in mentally?" Just to notice that you're in someone else's business can bring you back to your wonderful self. What a sweet place to be. Home.

There are no physical problems—only mental ones.

Depression, pain, and fear are gifts that say, "Sweetheart, take a look at your thinking in this moment. You're living in a story that isn't true for you." Living a lie is always stressful. And investigating a lie through The Work always leads you back to who you are. Who you are is not an option. You are love. It hurts to believe you're other than who you are, to live any story less than love.

I am you. I am so melded into you that when you breathe, it's my breath. When you sit, it's me sitting. You'll say something, and I am absolutely there at that moment. It's as if I own you and you own me. Your voice is my voice, literally. And it doesn't have any meaning for me, so that, without prejudice or separation, I can join it wherever you are.

The reason this speaks is because it does. If I thought I was doing it, I wouldn't be such a fool. My only purpose is to do what I'm apparently doing. When I do The Work with someone, my purpose is to sit with that person and ask the questions. If someone asks me a question, my purpose is to give my experience through my answer. I'm an effect of their suffering; there's no cause arising here. The cause is what people would call outside me, and their outside is my inside. When someone talks, I'm a listener. When someone asks, I'm a response.

Attachment to a thought means believing that the thought is true. When we don't inquire, we assume that a thought is true, though we can't ever know that. The purpose of attachment is to keep us from the realization that we are already truth. We don't attach to things; we attach to our stories about things.

Thoughts are friends, not enemies. They're just what is. They appear. They're innocent. We're not doing them. They're not personal. They're like the breeze or the leaves on the trees or the raindrops falling. Thoughts arise like that, and we can make friends with them. Would you argue with a raindrop? Raindrops aren't personal, and neither are thoughts. It's the meaning you attach to those thoughts that you think is personal. Inquire. Meet them with understanding. Once a painful concept is met with understanding, the next time it appears you may find it interesting. What used to be the nightmare is now just interesting. The next time it appears, you may find it funny. The next time, you may not even notice it. There will be no attachment. I meet thoughts the way I would meet my children. I meet them with love, gentleness, and a quiet understanding.

If you just understand "the three kinds of business" enough to stay in your own business, it could free your life in a way that you can't even imagine. The next time you're feeling stress or discomfort, ask yourself whose business you're in mentally, and you may burst out laughing! That question can bring you back to yourself. And you may come to see that you've never really been present, that you've been mentally living in other people's business all your life. And if you practice it for a while, you may come to see that *you* don't have any business either and that your life runs perfectly well on its own.

I do The Work with you because you think you need it. I don't have any such thought; I love you just the way you are. That's what I am to myself. You are my internal life. So your asking is my asking. It's just me asking myself for my own freedom. This is self-love. It's perfectly greedy, always.

When someone is facilitating The Work, giving the four questions, he's receiving at another level what I originally received inside me. If he's really facilitating from a neutral position, without any motive, then he's in the place where I am on the other side. It just gains in its freedom. It's in or out: unlimited.

Wherever you come from, I'll come from that same position in order to meet you. That's why there appears to be a contradiction in some of the things I say. I'm coming from different directions, and they're all true. Every vantage point is equal. It can sound like a direct retraction or like a puppy chasing its tail: it seems to go nowhere. It can sound like someone speaking in riddles. It can be confusing, and from one vantage point it can't be followed.

One of the wonderful things about The Work is that I can be talking with someone and he won't hear the paradox because we are so intimately joined, whereas to someone in the audience it may sound like gibberish. But if you're listening without thinking about what I mean—just letting yourself bathe in the experience of it, going inside and answering the questions for yourself, rather than waiting for the person in the chair to answer—you won't hear it as gibberish. It will make perfect sense.

People often ask me if I'm an enlightened being. I don't know anything about that. I'm just someone who knows the difference between *this hurts* and *this doesn't*. I'm someone who only wants what is. Meeting as a friend each concept that arose turned out to be my freedom. That's where The Work begins and ends—in me. The Work says, "Love it all, exactly as it is." And it shows you how. Wisdom is simply knowing the difference between what hurts and what doesn't hurt. There's immense freedom in that. It doesn't mean you have to do the right thing. It just allows you to stop fooling yourself and to do what you do with some awareness. One way leads to suffering; the other way leads to peace.

The world is your perception of it. Inside and outside always match—they're reflections of each other. The world is the mirror image of your mind. If you experience chaos and confusion inside, your external world has to reflect that. You have to see what you believe, because you are the confused thinker looking out and seeing yourself. You're the interpreter of everything, and if you're chaotic, what you hear and see has to be chaos. Even if Jesus, even if the Buddha, were standing in front of you and speaking, you'd only hear confused words, because confusion would be the listener. You'd only hear what you thought he was saying, and you'd start arguing with him the first time your story was threatened.

God's will and my will are the same, whether I notice it or not.

To think that you know what's best for another person is to be out of your business. The result is worry, anxiety, and fear. When you mentally step out of your business, you think that you know more than he, she, or God. The only real question is "Can I know what's right for myself?" That is your only business. And, as you eventually come to see, not even that.

What I love about The Work is that we come to see that both states—what we call bliss and what we call ordinary—are equal. One state isn't higher than the other. There's nothing to strive for anymore, nothing to leave behind. That's the beauty of inquiry—it doesn't matter where we are, it's all good.

Teacher is not a word that I would use to describe myself, although I respect it. You ask me a question, I answer you, you hear what you think I say, and you set yourself free. I am your projection. I am, for you, no more and no less than your story of me. You tell the story of how I'm wonderful or how I'm terrible. You see me as an enlightened being and make me into an all-knowing guru and fairy godmother, or you see me as a New Age spiritual flake, or you see me as a friend. What I want is for you to see me the way you see me. That's where the value is. You give me to yourself or you take me from yourself. I just want what you want.

The word *teacher* implies that we don't all teach equally or have equal wisdom. And that's not true. Everyone has equal wisdom. It's absolutely equally distributed. No one is wiser than anyone else. There's no one who can teach you except yourself.

The privilege of not having a teacher is that there's no tradition, so there's nothing to attach to. This one doesn't have to look like anything but what it is. It's just such a fool—it doesn't know anything but love. It's God delighted. It comes to take the mystery and importance out of everything. It takes the push and the time out of it.

You can't make a wrong decision; you can only experience the story arising about how *you* made it. I like to ask, "Are you breathing yourself?" No? Well, maybe you're not thinking yourself or making decisions either. Maybe it doesn't move until it moves, like a breath, like the wind. And you tell the story of how you are doing it, so you can keep yourself from the awareness that you are nature, flowing perfectly. Who would you be without the story that you need to make a decision? If it's your integrity to make a decision, make it. And guess what? In five minutes, you might change your mind and call it "you" again.

I like speaking from the earth place. I like what I call my disguise. The first thing I did when I woke up was to fall in love with form. I fell in love with the eyes and the floor and the ceiling. I am that. I am that. I am that. It's nothing, and it's everything. I love earth. I love the body of me. None of it is separate. Just to be born into it with eyes open is enough. Just to be born, now, into this goodness.

Whenever you invite me, I'll jump into your dream. I don't have a reason not to. I'll follow you through the tunnel, into the darkness, into the pit of hell. I'll go there, and I'll take you by the hand, and we'll walk through it together into the light. There's no place I won't go. I'm everything, everywhere. It's all a dream. I'll show you. That's what's so sweet about the four questions—they don't care what the story is. They just wait for you to ask them.

It's common for me to speak from the position of a personality, from the position of mankind, from the position of the earth, from the position of God, from the position of a rock. And I'll call myself "it," because I don't have a reference point for separation. I am all those things, and I don't have any concept that I'm not. I've simply learned to speak in a way that doesn't alienate people. It leaves me as benign, unseen, unknown. It leaves me as a comfortable place for people. I speak to them from the position of a friend, and people trust me because I meet them wherever they are. How do I do that? I'm in love.

I'm in passionate, blissful love. It's a love affair with itself. To meet people where they are, without any conditions, is to meet my own self without conditions. It's the simplest thing in the world. I'm always intoxicated with this love affair. I'm in love with everything. It's total vanity. I would kiss the ground I walk on—it's all me. But to kiss the ground would draw attention to itself. That's what the first three years after I woke up looked like. It's subtler now, more invisible. It has matured.

Decisions are easy. It's the story you tell about them that isn't easy. When you jump out of a plane and you pull the parachute cord and it doesn't open, you feel fear, because you have the next cord to pull. So you pull that one and it doesn't open. And that's the last cord. Now there's no decision to make. When there's no decision, there's no fear, so just enjoy the trip! And that's my position—I'm a lover of what is. What is: no cord to pull. It's already happening. Free fall. I have nothing to do with it.

I'm a lover of reality, because I know the freedom and power of being that. All I want is what is. That's it. My plan to change things could only leave me with less. Even a simple thought like "I'm not okay" can be depressing, because it's a flat-out lie. Even on my deathbed, I'm okay.

My own experience is that I live in completeness, and that we all do. It's the peace I walk in. I don't know anything. I don't have to figure anything out. I gave up forty-three years of thinking that went nowhere, and now I can be in the don't-know mind. This leaves nothing but peace and joy in my life. It's the absolute fulfillment of watching everything unfold in front of me as me.

Any story that you tell about yourself causes suffering. There is no authentic story.

What is God's intention? Whose business is God's intention? To go mentally into God's business is to be immediately lonely. That is why I keep that solid center—God is everything, God is good. I know his intention; it's exactly what is, in every moment. In fact, *God* is another name for what is. I don't have to question it anymore; it's over. I don't have to be outside myself, meddling in God's business. It's simple. God is everything, God is good. And from that basis it's clear that everything is perfect. Then, if we investigate, we lose even that. And that is intimacy. That is God itself. One with. One as. Itself.

It's not your job to like me—it's mine.

The four questions unraveled each story, and the turnaround led back to the storyteller—me. I am the storyteller. I become the story I tell myself. And I am what lives prior to every story. Every story, every thing, is God: reality. It apparently emerges from out of Itself, and appears as a life. It lives forever within the story, until the story ends. From out of Itself I appeared as my story, until the questions brought me home. I love it that inquiry is so unfailing. Story: pain; investigation: no story. Freedom is possible in every moment. This is The Work, the great undoing.

I stand as an untapped resource. What I'm here for is to bring this antivirus that I call The Work to those who think it would serve them. It's not for everyone. It's just an offering. That's what can be of use. Not my words, not my presence, nothing about me is of value. What is of value can't be seen or heard. I'm invisible. But what is manifest are the four questions and the turnaround. That's where the value is. That's what can be experienced when people are tired of suffering. They can reach out and have that, because it is their very own. Whenever it seems personal, as if I'm the one who has it, no one can accept it, because there *is* nothing personal, and they know this deep inside. They can use the questions and find themselves. The questions are the path back to our self. That's where I can be understood. I am you in the answers. At the center, that's where we meet. It's the only way I can be seen, heard, or understood: at the center, the heart, the truth. I'm only born to people there.

When we love what is, it becomes so simple to live in the world. The world is exactly as it should be.

Everything is God. Everything is good. We're always going to get what we need, not what we think we need. Then we come to see that what we need is not only what we have, it's what we want. Then we come to want only what is. That way, we always win, no matter what.

My experience is that I'm free. It's how I live internally. I have investigated my thinking, and I discovered that it doesn't mean a thing. I shine with the joy of understanding. I know about suffering, and I know about joy, and I know who I am. I am goodness. That's who we all are. There's no harm here. I would extinguish myself before I would step on an ant intentionally, because I know how to live. With no story, there's nothing to worry about. When there's nothing to do, nowhere to go, no one to be, no past or future, everything feels right. It's all good.

What does compassion look like? At a funeral, just eat the cake! You don't have to know what to do. It's revealed to you. Someone will come into your arms. It speaks. You're not doing it. Compassion isn't a doing.

Don't bother thinking about it; just eat the cake. If you're connected through pain, you're just standing or you're sitting. And if there's no pain, you're still just standing or sitting. But one way you're comfortable, the other way you're not.

Only in this moment (which doesn't exist) are you in reality. Everyone can learn to live in the moment, *as* the moment, to love what is in front of you, to love it as you. The miracle of love comes to you in the presence of the uninterpreted moment. If you are mentally somewhere else, you miss real life.

I experience everything in slow motion. More accurately, I experience everything frame by frame by frame. It's like looking at the comics in the newspaper. You see one frame saying this and the next one saying that. For me, each word is a frame. Each moment is a frame. Each frame is a universe in itself, not connected with any other. It's everything in itself. It's like the rock with lichen on it that you look at through a magnifying glass: a universe in itself, completely undivided.

When I'm walking, each movement within one step is complete in itself. It's one step at a time, but actually it's everything in between that, too. Now. Now. Now. Now. There is literally no time and space, no past or future or present, even, no one coming, no one going. It's just this, as it is—now. There's no meaning to it, no motive in it. And finally you get to a place where nothing moves. That is home, the place we all long for, the still point, the center of the universe, absolute zero.

When something's over, it's over. We all know when that point comes, and we can honor it or ignore it. When my hand reaches out for a cup of tea, I lavish myself on the whole cup of tea, even though I don't know if I'm going to finish one sip, three sips, ten sips, or the whole cup.

Someone gave me a precious gift the other day, and I loved it. But the gift was in the receiving. In that it was over, and I noticed that I gave it away immediately. Its purpose was over. There's no value to even the most precious object beyond the giving and receiving.

There's such abundance here, now, always. There's a table. There's a floor. There's a rug on the floor. There's a window. There's a sky. A sky! There are two friends—not one, not zero, but two. I could go on and on describing the world I live in now. It would take a lifetime to describe this moment, this now, which doesn't even exist except as my story. And isn't it beautiful? Reality as it is. It just is. I could die in such abundance, and I didn't do anything for it but notice.

We buy a home for our children, for our bodies; we get a garage for our car; we have doghouses for our dogs; but we won't give the mind a home. We treat it like an outcast. We shame it and blame it and shame it again. But if you let the mind ask its questions, then the heart will reveal the answers. Then the mind can finally rest at home in the heart and come to see that it and the heart are one.

That's what these four questions are about. You write down the problem and investigate, and the heart gives you the answer you've always known.

This is humility. There's nothing else to do. Standing in a room or sitting in a chair, just watch the story. If it's frightening or depressing, ask four questions, turn it around, and come home.

Just let it be. You may as well; it is. Everything moves in and out at its own time. You have no control. You've never had any; you never will. You only tell the story of what you think is happening. Do you think you cause movement? You don't. It just apparently is, but you tell the story of how you had something to do with it. "*I* moved my legs. *I* decided to walk." I don't think so. Inquire and see that it's just a story about what is. You know that you're going to move because everything is happening simultaneously. You tell the story before the movement, because you already are that. *It* moves, and you think that you did it. Then you tell the story of how you're going somewhere or how you're doing something. The only place you can play with is the story. That's the only game in town.

Some people think that compassion means feeling another person's pain. That's nonsense. It's not possible to feel another person's pain. You imagine what you'd feel if you were in that person's shoes, and you feel your own projection. Who would you be without your story? Pain-free, happy, and totally available if someone needs you—a listener, a teacher in the house, a Buddha in the house, the one who lives it.

As long as you think there's a you and a me, let's get the bodies straight. What I love about separate bodies is that when you hurt, I don't—it's not my turn. And when I hurt, you don't. Can you be there for me without putting your own suffering between us? Your suffering can't show me the way. Suffering can only teach suffering.

Without a teacher there was no one to tell me that thought was an enemy. So it was only natural that eventually I would meet each thought with understanding and welcome it as a friend. I can't meet you as an enemy and not feel it. So how could I meet a thought within me as an enemy and not feel it? When I learned to meet my thinking as a friend, I noticed that I met every human as a friend. What could you say about me that I haven't thought already? It's so simple.

There's no suffering in the world; there's only an uninvestigated story that leads you to believe it. There's no suffering in the world that's real. Isn't that amazing! Do The Work and come to know it for yourself.

We only fear what we are—what we haven't gone inside and taken a look at and met with understanding. If I think you might see me as boring, it would frighten me, because I haven't investigated that thought. So it's not people who frighten me, it's me that frightens me. That's my job, until I investigate and stop this fear for myself. The worst that can happen is that I think you think about me what I think about myself. So I am sitting in a pool of me.

When you become a lover of what is, the war is over. No more decisions to make. I like to say, "I'm a woman with no future." When there are no decisions to make, there's no future. All my decisions are made for me, as they're all made for you. You're just mentally telling the story of how you have something to do with it.

Until there's peace within you, there is no peace in the world, because you are the world, you are the earth. The story of earth is all there is of earth and beyond. When you're in dreamless sleep at night, is there a world? Not until you open your eyes and say "I": "I woke up," "I have to go to work," "I'm going to brush my teeth." Until "I" is born, there's no world. When the I arises, welcome to the movie of who you think you are. Get the popcorn, here it comes! But if you investigate it, there's no attachment. It's just a great movie. And if you don't investigate, the I arises and it's body-identified, and you think it's real. That's pure fantasy. If you think you're that, you may want to inquire.

You can't have it because you already *are* it. You already have what you want. You already are what you want. This is as good as it gets. It appears as this now. Perfect. Flawless. And to argue with that is to experience the lie. The Work can give you this wonderful awareness: the awareness of the lie and the power of truth. The beauty of what really is.

Don't pretend yourself beyond your evolution.

You don't experience anxiety unless you've attached to a thought that isn't true for you. It's that simple. You don't ever feel anxiety until you believe that a thought is true—and it's not.

There is a sweetness about the earth. I call it reality. Someone once referred to me as the master of descension. He said, "I've heard of masters of ascension, but you are the master of descension." So, because I had no teacher, I had nothing to aspire to. It was easy to fall in love with what is: woman sitting in chair with cup of tea. That's as sweet as I want it, because that is what is. When you love what is, it becomes so simple to live in the world, because the world is exactly as it should be.

We are really alive when we live in nonbelief—open, waiting, trusting, and loving to do what appears in front of us now.

People talk about self-realization, and this is it! Can you just breathe in and out? To hell with enlightenment! Just enlighten yourself in this moment. Can you just do that? And then, eventually, it all collapses. The mind finds a home in the heart. The mind merges with the heart and comes to see that it's not separate. It finds a home and it rests. It can't be threatened or scolded or frightened away. Until the story is met with understanding, there is no peace. Only love and understanding heal.

Mind appears to flow everywhere, but it is the unmoving, the never having-moved. It appears as everything. Eventually it sees that nowhere is where it is. Its unceasing work is self-realization. It feels humble, because it sees that what hasn't been created can't be claimed. The splendor of humility is all that it's left with. It's left in a state of gratitude for everything: for itself.

The ego is terrified of the truth. And the truth is that the ego doesn't exist.

The Work always leaves you with less of a story. Who would you be without your story? You never know until you inquire. There is no story that is you or that leads to you. Every story leads away from you. Turn it around; undo it. You are what exists before all stories. You are what remains when the story is understood.

Someone says, "Oh, it's a terrible day; I'm so depressed." He's the champion of suffering, saying that there's something wrong here, something less than beauty. He's the mirror image without a clue that he's just a mirror image. Just be the is, the story-less movement, the reflection—nothing more. And in that, the source is known and merged. The reflection moves as God, without argument. And that is awareness, the joy of what people call the world and what I refer to as the image of God Itself dancing. Every story of a problem, when it is investigated, becomes laughable. And even that is God.

I'll say things like, "Until I'm free to be happy in the presence of my worst enemy, my Work's not done." And people can hear that as a motive for doing The Work. It's not—it's an observation. If you do The Work with some kind of motive—of getting your wife back or getting sober—forget it! Do The Work for the love of truth, for the love of freedom. Isn't that what you want your wife for anyway? So that you can be happy and free? Well, skip the middleman and be happy and free now! You're it. You're the one. There's nothing else to do.

People ask how I can live if nothing has any meaning and I'm no one. It's very simple. We are being lived. We're not doing it. Are you breathing yourself? That's the end of the story. Did *you* just put your hand on your face? Did you plan it? Without a story, we move effortlessly, in perfect health, fluidly, freely, with a lot of love, and without war, without resistance. This possibility can be very frightening for people who think that they have control. Investigate, and see how life goes on, so much more joyfully. Even in its apparent collapsing, I see only joy.

If you knew how important you are—and without the story you come to know it—you would fragment into a billion pieces and just be light. That's what these misunderstood concepts are for: to keep you from the awareness of that. You'd have to be the embodiment if you knew it—just a fool, blind with love. It causes so much pain to live out of the light. I don't know how people do it for so long. It was so painful that I could only do it for forty-three years. Forty-three centuries.

Your ego has to terrify you all the time, so that you can investigate and come home to yourself in the body. This is what we're all here to live. When we aren't attached to our thinking, when all the why's, when's, and where's let go of us, then what really is becomes visible.

The fear of death is the last smokescreen for the fear of love. The mind looks at nothing and calls it something, to keep from experiencing what it really is. Every fear is the fear of love, because to discover the truth of anything is to discover that there is nobody, no doer, no me to create suffering or to identify with anything. Without any of that, there is just love.

Self meeting itself—that's the deal. If I wait for God to enlighten me, it could be a long wait—years, decades maybe. When I'm on my knees praying to God in all sincerity, *I'm* the one listening. Can I do what I've begged God to do? Can I hear myself? Who else is listening? I'm a lover of reality. Can I just listen to myself? And when I hear myself, there's no separation. If I want God to do something, I turn it around. And in the peace of that, I come to know the truth.

Live in the now? Even the thought "now" is a concept. Before the thought completes itself, it's gone, with no proof that it ever existed. Even thought doesn't exist. That's why everyone already has the quiet mind that they're seeking.

All pleasure is pain, until I understand. Then I am the pleasure I was seeking. I am what I always wanted. Pleasure is a mirror image of what we already have before we look away from what really is. When we stop seeking pleasure, the beauty concealed by the seeking becomes evident. It's so simple and clear. What we wanted to find from pleasure is simply what is left beyond all stories.

There is no beginning of time, only beginning of thought.

The illusion is the mirror image attaching to a belief. The illusion is the ego thinking that it's separate. It's not. It goes where God goes. God—reality—is all of it. The ego has no options. It can protest all it wants, but if God moves, it moves.

To me, reality is God, because it rules. How do I know that my brother should have died? He did. That's reality. That's what is. It doesn't wait for my vote or my opinion. And even that doesn't exist, because what is is the story of a past. What I love most about a story of the past is that it's over. That's why I'm a lover of reality. It's always kinder than the story.

The voice within is what I honor. It's what I'm married to. This life doesn't belong to me. The voice says, "Brush your teeth." Okay. I don't know what for, I just move on through. It says, "Walk." Okay. I just keep moving. Someone says, "Will you come do The Work with us?" Okay. I'm just following orders. The beautiful thing about this is that it's fun. If I don't follow the order, it's okay, too. This is a game about where it will take me if I do follow.

For forty-three years I was at war out in the story. And then one day, in a moment of clarity, I found my way back home. And that's what inquiry is all about. It comes from source, and it returns to source. It's such a gift. I was always merging into my stories, into my insanity. And then, one day, when I heard "Brush your teeth," it started coming back, and there was a receiver. And it opened, like a womb. It opened into that allowing, into the mystery. Each moment—new! "Brush your teeth." It doesn't sound very spiritual to me, but that's all it said. "Walk." It just opens and it becomes more of a listener. All marriage is nothing more than a metaphor of that marriage. And if I don't follow, if I tell it, "Later," I don't feel very comfortable. And then I come back and I brush my teeth. It becomes a thing that's timeless, because when you're opening to that, there's no time and space in it. It's just a "Yes. Yes. Yes." That's why I say, "Boundaries are an act of selfishness." I don't have any. When it says, "Jump," I jump. Because where I jump, I have nothing to lose. There's nothing more fun than following such an insane thing and saying "Yes" to it. You don't have anything to lose. You're dead already. You can afford to be a fool.

Every word is the sound of God. Every word is the word of God. There is nothing personal here. And everything is personal. If the moon rises, it's for you. You're the one watching it! (And that's just a beginning.)

The litmus test for self-realization is the constant state of gratitude. This gratitude is not something a person can look for or find. It comes from another direction. It takes us over completely. It's so vast that it can't be dimmed or overlaid. It's like its own self. The short version would be: God intoxicated with God, Itself. The total acceptance and consumption of Itself reflected back in the same moment in that central place that is like fusion. It's the beginning. What looks like the end is the beginning. And when you think life is so good that it can't get any better, it gets better. It has to. That's a law.

It's personal and it's not personal. It's personal in that the whole world is me—a mirror image that I am and love. Without it, I'm bodiless. And it's not that I need to look, it's just that looking is such a delight. On the other hand, it's not personal, because I see nothing more than a mirror image. Until God— reality—moves, I have no movement. Every movement, every sound, every breath, every molecule, every atom is nothing more than a mirror image of God. So I don't move, I'm being moved. I don't do, I'm being done. I don't think, I'm being thought. I don't breathe, I'm being breathed. There is no me, there is nothing personal or real about it. Whenever you speak, it's God speaking. When a flower blooms, it's God. When Hitler marches, it's God. I see only God. Add one more *o* and you've got *good*. To me they're synonymous. How could I not love all that I am, all that you are? One me.

If you find the internal work exciting, you'll come to look forward to the worst that can happen, because you won't find a problem that can't be healed from the inside. And you'll wonder how you ever thought there was a problem—ever. This is paradise found.

Forgiveness is discovering that what you thought happened, didn't—that there was never anything to forgive. No one has ever done anything terrible. There is nothing terrible except your thoughts about what you see. So whenever you suffer, inquire, look at the thoughts you're thinking, and set yourself free. Be a child. Know nothing. Follow your ignorance all the way to your freedom.

I experience the I arising, and I quake with the privilege of that, because the I is Its very self, being born. When the I arises, It is presenting Itself to Itself. Your name is the name of God. It's equal to "table." "I." "God."

We're not doing anything. Ultimately, we are being done. If I say, "I'm going to the store," I'm very clear that I am God going to God. *Store* is a word for God. *I* is a word for God. And *God* is a word for what is. When I say "I love you," there's no personality talking. It's self-love: I'm only talking to myself. The way I experience it is that It is only talking to Itself. If I say, "Let me pour you some tea," It is pouring Its own tea for Itself, and the tea is Itself. It's so self-absorbed that It leaves no room for any other. Nothing. Not a molecule separate from Itself. That's true love. It's the ultimate self. There's no other existence. It's self-consuming always and loving it. It's a guiltless state. There's no one separate. In the apparent world of duality, people are going to see it as a you and a me, but in reality there is only one. And even that's not true.

"Something is better than nothing"—is that true? *Something*—a word for God. *Nothing*—a word for God. They're the same. There's no preference. Haven't you noticed? Every word is a word for God. If you attach meaning to a word, welcome to genesis.

Everything is equal. There is no this soul or that soul. There's only one. And that's the last story. There's only one. And not even that. It doesn't matter how you attempt to be disconnected, it's not a possibility. Any thought you believe is an attempt to break the connection. But it's only an attempt; it can't be done. That's why it feels so uncomfortable.

Even so-called truths eventually fall away. Every truth is a distortion of what is. The last truth—I call it the last judgment—is "God is everything, God is good." Ultimately even this isn't true. But as long as it works for you, I say keep it and have a wonderful life.

211

We live as awareness, and awareness always focuses on something, because it's everything. It will notice its own finger or foot. Somewhere within it, there's always a focus. Its breath may surf the back of its tongue. It doesn't matter where the awareness is—the breath, the fingers, the toes—something is going on all the time within it, as it. There's nothing moving it, and yet it's in perpetual motion. Its focus is itself. It is always present, like your heartbeat. It doesn't go faster or slower. It's a steady condition. It's nothing, and it's so beautiful that it wants to call itself "something." Now it's a hand on my head, my elbow on the couch, my heart beating, my toes swaying to its natural rhythm. I notice that my fingers are doing the same, ever so slightly. It would be undetectable if I were attached to anything. And as I speak, the movement continues. There's no sound, even though it appears that I'm talking. When I hear sound, it is silence, also. The tongue hitting the roof of the mouth. Lips coming together as it speaks. The chair holding me. I am always held. Even in the walking, the earth holds me.

ACKNOWLEDGMENTS

I would like to express my love and deep gratitude to Prem Rikta, Michele Penner, Ellen Mack, Michael Katz, Josh Baran, Paula Brittain, Melony Malouf, Mischelle Miller, Lesley Pollitt, Bob Brittain, Penfield Chester, and all the staff members who have made the School for The Work possible for so many.

ABOUT THE AUTHOR

Byron Katie simple yet powerful method of inquiring into the cause of all our suffering is called The Work. Since 1986, Katie has introduced The Work to hundreds of thousands of people throughout the world at free public events; in prisons, hospitals, churches, corporations, universities, and schools; at weekend intensives; and at her nine-day School for The Work.

She is the author of the best-selling books *Loving What Is, I Need Your Love—Is That True?,* and *A Thousand Names for Joy.* Her Website is **www.TheWork.com**, where you can find her blog, her schedule, a network of facilitators of The Work, a free hotline, audio and video clips, articles, and basic information.

Visit **www.TheWork.com** and change your life:

- Learn more about **The Work.**
- Download **audio and video clips of Katie** doing The Work with others.
- Print out **Worksheets** for daily use.
- Establish a practice on the **NetWork**, find a **facilitator**, or call the free **hotline.**
- See Katie's **schedule of events.**
- Join Katie's **Parlor.**
- Find out about the nine-day **School for The Work with Byron Katie.**
- Visit the store for Katie's **books**, **CDs**, and **DVDs.**

We hope you enjoyed this Hay House book. If you'd like to receive a free catalog featuring additional Hay House books and products, or if you'd like information about the Hay Foundation, please contact:

Hay House, Inc.
P.O. Box 5100
Carlsbad, CA 92018-5100

(760) 431-7695 or **(800) 654-5126**
(760) 431-6948 (fax) or **(800) 650-5115 (fax)**
www.hayhouse.com® • **www.hayfoundation.org**

Published and distributed in Australia by: Hay House Australia Pty. Ltd., 18/36 Ralph St., Alexandria NSW 2015 • *Phone:* 612-9669-4299 *Fax:* 612-9669-4144 • www.hayhouse.com.au

Published and distributed in the United Kingdom by: Hay House UK, Ltd., 292B Kensal Rd., London W10 5BE • *Phone:* 44-20-8962-1230 *Fax:* 44-20-8962-1239 • www.hayhouse.co.uk

Published and distributed in the Republic of South Africa by: Hay House SA (Pty), Ltd., P.O. Box 990, Witkoppen 2068 • *Phone/Fax:* 27-11-467-8904 orders@psdprom.co.za • www.hayhouse.co.za

Published in India by: Hay House Publishers India, Muskaan Complex, Plot No. 3, B-2, Vasant Kunj, New Delhi 110 070 • *Phone:* 91-11-4176-1620 • *Fax:* 91-11-4176-1630 • www.hayhouse.co.in

Distributed in Canada by: Raincoast, 9050 Shaughnessy St., Vancouver, B.C. V6P 6E5 • *Phone:* (604) 323-7100 *Fax:* (604) 323-2600 • www.raincoast.com

Tune in to **HayHouseRadio.com®** for the best in inspirational talk radio featuring top Hay House authors! And, sign up via the Hay House USA Website to receive the Hay House online newsletter and stay informed about what's going on with your favorite authors. You'll receive bimonthly announcements about Discounts and Offers, Special Events, Product Highlights, Free Excerpts, Giveaways, and more! **www.hayhouse.com®**